In the ebb and flow of life there are moments that make us *stop*, making phones fall silent and quick solutions impossible; moments brought about by the unthinkable: a diagnosis that reads like a death sentence, an unrecoverable economic disaster, an unbearable loss. You find yourself hurled to the crossroads of your faith. *What do you believe?* Tish Hagee Tucker has answered this age-old question as she shares her moment and those of others: God is FOR you. God is a HEALER, a RESTORER, and He will NEVER change. You will be blessed by this anointed book!

—SYBEL M. PICI
OWNER/OPERATOR, PICICO DBA MCDONALD'S

Tish Hagee Tucker knows firsthand what it's like to face a formidable giant and walk away triumphant. Her story, as well as those of friends and family along the way, gives witness to God's tender mercies and His magnificent healing power. It's a reminder to us all that no matter who you are, no matter what your circumstance, God is the master of EVERY situation, and He specializes in the impossible.

—TANYA GOODMAN SYKES
GOSPEL MUSIC HALL OF FAME

I've known Tish since our teenage years, and the one thing I can unashamedly say is that she is real and she speaks from the heart of her experiences. She writes about what she has lived and experienced, not just what she has learned from someone (usually her dad or brother) in the pulpit. She has tried and tested those promises of God, and HE has always come through. She knew me when I was miraculously healed my sophomore year in high school. God is real! Tish has a way of writing that can bring you into the experience like no other author I know. You will laugh with her, cry with her, and rejoice with her, but what I hope is that you see the same God she knows and experience Him in your own life without limitation.

—KIMBERLY WRAY
VP, CLEAR CHANNEL COMMUNICATIONS

Tish has been through the valley of the shadow of death and has come out to tell us, "I made it and you can too." God knows that we need people to bring hope to us when hope seems so far. I have heard her testimony, and WOW! This young mom, wife, sister, friend, daughter, and businesswoman found the Healing Master. I know this book will give you hope and is written by a person who has been made transparent.

—YVONNE POGUE
SOUTH TEXAS CHRISTIAN CENTER
WOMEN'S AGLOW TEXAS CHAPTER

While most of us spend our lives being a *work in progress* and crawling along in search of maturity in faith, Tish is leading the marathon and taking leaps into the abyss, always confident that she will land in God's gentle embrace. Those of us who pay attention to Tish's travels through life know that we have but to sit back, watch, and learn. She has wisdom in the face of wickedness and graceful calm in the throes of calamity. If you ever doubted that God has warriors on this earth, you haven't met

Tish! This book is yet one more testimony to the strength of believing...can't wait for the next one!
—ANNETTE CRAVEN, PHD

Master of the Impossible is truly an inspiration to edify and comfort believers. An honest reveal of how human nature causes all of us to think that we can handle our own problems before we ask God for His help. God only asked that we love Him and obey His commandments. With God's help we need not be afraid of tomorrow because He is already there. Our submission is our gift to God, and He will be faithful to our needs. This wonderful book is full of stories about obedience to God's Word. Thank you, Tish, for sharing your story of God's love and faithfulness in such a beautiful way.
—VAN MABEE
THE MABEE FOUNDATION

Every life will face "impossibles." With profound insight and signature authenticity Tish Hagee Tucker brings us *Master of the Impossible*. Empowering, encouraging, and inspiring—this is a message for every life and every "impossible." Introduce your impossible to the Master.
—DONDI SCUMACI
AUTHOR, *DESIGNED FOR SUCCESS, CAREER MOVES,*
AND *READY, SET...GROW*

Tish Hagee Tucker has a wit and wisdom about her that are contagious. As you read, you feel like she's your friend and that she understands everything you're going through. That's because she's been there herself and come out on the other side with a stronger understanding of her faith and how God works. She lives and breathes her faith with conviction, and she pulls no punches when it's time to share the truth.

—LORI TWICHELL
OWNER/REVIEWER, RADIANT LIT AND
FICTIONADDICT.COM
OWNER, BEYOND THE BUZZ MARKETING

I have known Tish Hagee Tucker for more than thirty years and have watched her grow in faith and character. In tragedy and triumph, in harmony and heartache, in the face of fear and in the hand of faith, I have watched her stand her ground, laugh in adversity, and overcome with grace and joy. All who read her stories will be moved to tears, will laugh out loud, will be encouraged to stand in the face of adversity, and will overcome the challenges life can bring.

—IKE PAULI JR., MD

MASTER
OF THE
IMPOSSIBLE

MASTER
OF THE
IMPOSSIBLE

TISH HAGEE TUCKER

CHARISMA
HOUSE

Most CHARISMA HOUSE BOOK GROUP products are available at special quantity discounts for bulk purchase for sales promotions, premiums, fund-raising, and educational needs. For details, write Charisma House Book Group, 600 Rinehart Road, Lake Mary, Florida 32746, or telephone (407) 333-0600.

MASTER OF THE IMPOSSIBLE by Tish Hagee Tucker
Published by Charisma House
Charisma Media/Charisma House Book Group
600 Rinehart Road
Lake Mary, Florida 32746
www.charismahouse.com

Unless otherwise noted, all Scripture quotations are from the New King James Version of the Bible. Copyright © 1979, 1980, 1982 by Thomas Nelson, Inc., publishers. Used by permission.

Scripture quotations marked KJV are from the King James Version of the Bible.

Scripture quotations marked NIV are from the Holy Bible, New International Version. Copyright © 1973, 1978, 1984, International Bible Society. Used by permission.

Cover design by Justin Evans
Design Director: Bill Johnson

Library of Congress Cataloging-in-Publication Data:
An application to register this book for cataloging has been
submitted to the Library of Congress.
International Standard Book Number: 978-1-62136-217-3
E-book ISBN: 978-1-62136-218-0

While the author has made every effort to provide accurate
telephone numbers and Internet addresses at the time of
publication, neither the publisher nor the author assumes
any responsibility for errors or for changes that occur after
publication.

First edition

13 14 15 16 17 — 9 8 7 6 5 4 3 2 1
Printed in the United States of America

To a sweet young lady who bravely shared the triumphant story of how she overcame horrific tragedy. You will never know that you saved the lives of two beautiful little girls because of your powerful testimony and your willingness to share. May God bless you far above your ability to contain!

CONTENTS

ACKNOWLEDGMENTS

TO THOSE WHO have allowed me to share their most personal stories with others in order to encourage them through their own personal crises, I humbly thank you! To the many contributors to this manuscript, I am deeply touched by your kindness.

> "For I will surely deliver you, and you shall not fall by the sword; but your life shall be as a prize to you, because you have put your trust in Me," says the LORD.
>
> —JEREMIAH 39:18

FOREWORD

THE ONLY SIGNIFICANCE of life consists in helping to establish the kingdom of God on earth, and this can be done only by means and the acknowledgment of the living truth of God by each one of us.

My daughter Tish has just written her second book sharing some of the personal and gripping stories of crisis the Hagee family has faced and endured. These true-life stories present God as the Master of the impossible, as the God who is always there in a time of trouble, as a loving and gracious God who will never leave you or forsake you, even in your darkest hour.

Master of the Impossible is a great read and an exciting page-turner! If you're looking for something to encourage you to look up and try again, *Master of the Impossible* is a must-read!

—Pastor John Hagee
Senior pastor, Cornerstone Church
San Antonio, TX

INTRODUCTION

THE GRASS MIGHT look greener on the other side of the fence, and the problems your friends are handling might seem trivial in comparison to your own. But everyone has a story. None of us paddle through life on the USS *Painfree*.

If you have never been sick, how will you ever know the overwhelmingly wonderful sensation of life-sustaining healing? If you have never trudged through rain, how can you fully appreciate the spectrum of colors found in the rainbow? If you have never had a seemingly unsolvable problem, how can you relish the divine answer when it comes?

When life hands us the most impossibly ridiculous problem we never thought we would face, we have two choices: we can hang on to the problem for as long as we wish, trying to strategize with our limited resources, hacking out a plan of limited success. Or, if we are tired of trying to fight the giant on our own, we can ask God for His direction and rest assured that what is on the way is far greater than anything we could ever imagine. *Nothing* is too difficult for God.

No matter your age or the stage of life you are going through, God sees you. There is no place you can hide where He cannot count your tears. There is no place you can run that is too far from His reach. If you will only touch the hem of His garment and believe in Him, He will heal the part of you that is impossibly broken.

It is my prayer that after you have read this book, you understand how important it is to hand God the problems in your life, not a slice of the problem but the whole lousy thing. When we trust Him, He is faithful and just to bring us out to rich fulfillment. Don't walk around the same mountain until it has been reduced to an anthill. Wake up and say, "This is the day the LORD has made; [I] will rejoice and be made glad in it" (Ps. 118:24). Take the bull by the horns, and know that you have everything you need to be more than a conqueror in Jesus Christ. He is the Master of the impossible!

> Because he has set his love upon Me, therefore I
>   will deliver him;
> I will set him on high, because he has known My
>   name.
> He shall call upon Me, and I will answer him;
> I will be with him in trouble;
> I will deliver him and honor him.
> With long life I will satisfy him,
> And show him My salvation.
>
> —PSALM 91:14–16

Chapter 1

WHAT? ME? CANCER?

*Yea, though I walk through the valley of the
shadow of death, I will fear no evil; for You are
with me; Your rod and Your staff, they comfort me.*
—Psalm 23:4

HAVE YOU EVER had one of those days that was pure perfection? Sunshine is blinding you from every angle. A colorful array of birds perched outside your window ledge is singing your favorite tune. The most amazing job of your career was just dropped in your lap, or maybe you purchased the dream home that fulfills your wildest fantasy. All the while you are driving in a brand-new car that was ten thousand dollars off of the manufacturer's suggested retail price—today only. Your day couldn't possibly get any better—and then the phone rings.

Every one of us has a story—a culmination of life's highs and lows, a twisted journey carved into our existence that has shaped us into the person we are today. Every one of us has received *that* call—the one that left us breathless, shattering our hearts into a million tiny pieces. How could this possibly be happening to *us*?

This chapter is the story of *my* call.

1

The cell phone dropped like an anvil into my lap and slid to the floorboard of my car. All I could hear was the deafening sound of three words I will never forget if I live to be two hundred years old: "You have leiomyosarcoma."

The tiny sentence sucked me into a black vortex. A million questions fought to be answered, reverberating in a state of mass chaos inside my head: How did this happen? Are they sure they got the right diagnosis? I'm healthy. I don't even have serious allergies. Could a podiatrist really deliver a cancer diagnosis over the phone? While I'm driving down a highway nicknamed the Death Loop? Was this some kind of cruel joke?

And just like that my bronchitis diagnosis was upgraded to cancer. The rainbow I had been riding, full of lollipops and unicorns, had become a full-blown thundercloud— cloudy with a 100 percent chance of cancer. There was no part of my being that wasn't completely numb.

The feeling of someone literally handing you a death sentence is one of utter helplessness, as if everything you knew to be certain just moments ago is spiraling out of control. It's like being in a crowded mall and finding out there are only a few seconds left until the bomb left behind by terrorists is set to go off. There is no time to run for cover and no apparent shelter to avoid the pending danger.

Where do you turn when there is no sheltering place, when you cannot find any relief within the comfortable confines of your life? Where do you go when the impossible stares you in the face and you are fresh out of answers? To whom do you turn?

Healthy life as I had enjoyed it just seconds ago was over.

As I continued driving down the highway, random bits of

information flooded my brain, as if a million people were shouting, demanding my complete attention. In the middle of Satan telling me, "You just received a death sentence, so now what? I can control you through fear. Your life is over," I heard even more loudly these verses from Psalm 27:

> The LORD is my light and my salvation;
> Whom shall I fear?
> The LORD is the strength of my life;
> Of whom shall I be afraid?
> When the wicked came against me
> To eat up my flesh,
> My enemies and foes,
> They stumbled and fell.
> Though an army may encamp against me,
> My heart shall not fear;
> Though war may rise against me,
> In this I will be confident....
> He shall hide me in His pavilion;
> In the secret place of His tabernacle
> He shall hide me;
> He shall set me high upon a rock.
> —PSALM 27:1–3, 5

I pride myself on being a brilliant multitasker, but at that moment my brain was on complete overload. There was no compartmentalizing information. There was no logical sense behind any closed door. I was looking for a quick answer to a problem I could never solve on my own, and my brain felt like it was drowning in a lack of information. For the first time in my life I had no clue where to begin looking for a logical solution. There were no formidable answers in front of me, and my brain was desperately seeking a remedy.

The only thing I knew beyond a shadow of a doubt was that cancer is an incurable disease, and if God did not heal me, my life would surely end.

GATHERING THE PRAYER WARRIORS

My first response was to start calling family members. I could not digest the information I was about to relay to them, and yet the message was becoming louder and more prominent as the miles beneath my tires rolled away. I needed an immediate support group to help me make sense of the totally incomprehensible phone call I had just received. Please. Someone. Tell me that everything is going to be all right. Tell me *I'm* not the one who is sick.

I wasn't receiving a call about someone else. *My* phone was the one that was ringing, and it was a very odd and sobering experience. Where could I even begin? It was as if I was tasked with catching Moby Dick and given an inflatable canoe with Popsicle sticks for paddles.

I decided to call my dad, Pastor John Hagee of Cornerstone Church in San Antonio, Texas, because he can usually solve any problem in a matter of milliseconds. He can give you the answer for world peace while dictating a memo, watching newsreels, and writing up new ideas for upcoming projects...in the middle of a nap. He is a world-class problem solver, so it was no big surprise that I called him for advice.

When I rolled up to the front of his house in my Suburban, I was not ready for the look of complete shock on his face.

He was just as surprised as I was. In all my thirty-seven years I had never known my father to be at such a loss. At that moment the fact that I had an impossible situation on my hands sank in to my very bones. What was I going to do now?

Being raised as a pastor's daughter, I had been given the great luxury of learning about God's divine assistance my entire life. But really, do we call out for this wonderful tool when we think we can fix everything ourselves? Usually we try to repair or manipulate the broken parts of our lives, never tapping into this unlimited resource. After all, if we can fix it on our own, why bother God with petty details?

In my case there were only two brutal facts I knew for certain. Fact number one: I had been irrefutably diagnosed with leiomyosarcoma, a fact confirmed by a world-class team of doctors. There was no need for a second opinion. I had a rare cancer known to be extremely aggressive and unforgiving. Fact number two: there was no other place to turn for supernatural help other than Jehovah God.

Psalm 103:1–4 says, "Praise the LORD, O my soul…who forgives all your sins and heals all your diseases, who redeems your life from the pit and crowns you with love and compassion" (NIV). I desperately needed a healer for my disease, someone to save me from dying—not figuratively but literally.

Before I left my dad's house that day, he announced in his normal authoritative voice that could stop a freight train on a dime, "We are turning back to the Bible [Ps. 119:105]. God's Word and His promises have never failed us, and they will not fail us now." My family would circle me in prayer until I received total healing. Failure was not an option. And, if just for that brief moment, the circus in my head stopped and listened.

I went home carrying this overwhelming and utterly impossible situation on my shoulders, and yet I could already feel the prayers pouring in from all directions. I had no answers, and yet inexplicable peace was beginning to seep into the cracks of the chaos. Prayer is a powerful tool, second to none. When you know how to use it (and we will talk about this later in the book), there is no enemy that can defeat you.

"God, I Need You Now!"

As soon as I got home, my knees hit the hardwood floor. The weight of this problem was crushing me on every side, but I knew the answer was already on its way (2 Cor. 4:8–9). I did not ask God why I had cancer or how long I would be traveling down this road. I simply wanted to let Him know there was no way of surviving this cancer journey alone. I needed the Master of the impossible to lead the way. This was not a put-on-my-glittery-red-shoes-and-tap-my-way-down-the-yellow-brick-road situation. This was a full tilt GOD-I-NEED-YOU-NOW situation.

I wasn't bargaining with God, saying, "If You heal me, then I will..." I was simply getting my house in order. Sometimes healing means complete restoration here on earth, and sometimes healing means dying. At this point in my cancer career I wasn't sure which road I would be traveling in my dusty flip-flops. But I knew the road would not be easy. It was time to strap on my armor and get ready for whatever demons were coming my way (Eph. 6:10–11).

My number-one concern was my children. I was not

afraid to die, knowing I would be going to a place with no alarm clocks, no bills to pay, and no slow drivers in front of me in the fast lane. But what would happen to my baby girls? They were three and five years old at the time of my diagnosis and, thankfully, too young to understand the severity of my disease. This was a huge blessing for me to not have to carry the burden of my disease for them. They were blissfully unaware of the potentially horrific consequences.

As I began praying that evening, my girls were at the forefront of my mind. When my prayer began, I asked God to forgive me of all of my sins. I didn't think God had given me cancer because of something I had done; I simply wanted to come before Him with a clean slate. Then I began to very clearly lay out how desperate I was for a healing touch and how much I needed God to place a hedge of protection around my children—emotionally, physically, and spiritually.

Next I asked God to grant me a stay of execution if my daughters' lives would in any way be negatively impacted or if they would blame God for losing me at such a young age. I did not want to be the reason they didn't fulfill their divine destinies. I wanted to lead them down the right path for many decades to come. I was asking God to show me unmerited mercy.

Finally, as Psalm 103 says, I began to praise the Lord. I have found that when you are praising, there is no room for doubt and fear. Since I had absolutely nothing to lose and everything to gain, I started praising the Lord and asking God to spare my life and allow me to continue living with my two precious daughters. It was a lot to ask, but I had no doubt God was able to not only meet but also exceed the expectations of this life-altering request.

I began singing one song after another. As soon as something popped into my mind, I started singing and praising, knowing that all I could do was tell God that my time was in His hands. Whatever the consequences, I would praise Him through the good and the bad (Ps. 34:1). I would be thankful for whatever time I had left. I sang until I had no voice left and I was completely exhausted on every possible level. I was so tired it hurt to blink, and at the same time I was filled with great expectation.

The Holy Spirit saturated my bedroom like a thick, suffocating fog. When God is right next to you, there is no mistaking it. He said, "Grab a pen, kid, and take some notes. This is going to be *really* good."

Psalm 61 was the answer I was given to my insurmountable problem:

> Hear my cry, O God;
> Attend to my prayer.
> From the end of the earth I will cry to You,
> When my heart is overwhelmed;
> Lead me to the rock that is higher than I.
> For You have been a shelter for me,
> A strong tower from the enemy.
> I will abide in Your tabernacle forever;
> I will trust in the shelter of Your wings. Selah.
> For You, O God, have heard my vows;
> You have given me the heritage of those who fear
> Your name.
> You will prolong the king's life,
> His years as many generations.
> He shall abide before God forever.

Oh, prepare mercy and truth, which may preserve
    him!
So I will sing praise to Your name forever,
That I may daily perform my vows.

That night I fell asleep knowing God would be with me every step of the way. I had total peace and slept like a baby. There was no logical reason for me *not* to worry, but I knew God saw me and was already sending His angels to cover me...before the very first utterance that came out of my mouth.

The next morning I awoke still laminated by a thick layer of unanswered questions that again formed a jumbled mess rattling around in my mind. I was fighting to wrap my mind around my new existence. While the face in the mirror looked exactly the same as it did yesterday, I knew this was a totally different person staring back at me.

At this point I didn't know the extent of my disease, but I knew the unlimited power of my Healer. And for this fragmented moment in time, that had to be enough. The battle belonged to the Lord.

BENEFACTORS ON EVERY LEVEL

As time has passed, I have thought about the finer details of that evening, alone in my bedroom, just God and me. That night set the standard of confidence that would follow me throughout my cancer journey. I was not afraid because I had a very strong support system constantly holding me up in prayer. I didn't doubt God would come through for me because He had already given me the perfect promise in Psalm 61. All I had to do was wait and watch for God's plan to come to fruition. But why would God want to help *me*? What was in it for God?

The truth of the matter is that *we* are the benefactors on every level. God can clearly exist without us, but we cannot exist without Him. Some of my favorite aspects of God are His loving kindness and mercy. According to Webster's dictionary, *mercy* comes from the Latin word for "price paid." *Grace* comes from "favor." The definition for *mercy* is "a blessing that is an act of divine favor or passion." Another passage calls it "unmerited divine assistance." (And yes, this is the regular Webster's dictionary, not a seminary adaptation.) I had done nothing, and yet He was *still* willing to help me.

Lamentations 3:22–23 says, "Through the LORD's mercies we are not consumed, because His compassions fail not. They are new every morning; great is Your faithfulness."

To me this means that if I was diagnosed with cancer every single day, God would be ready to go to bat for me. Every single morning when I woke up, He would be ready to fight my battles for me. I can imagine Him saying, "Come on, kid. Get out of bed. I've got this day completely taken care of for you. All you need to do is listen to Me, and I will show you some amazing things. No need to worry." (See Psalm 37:23.) He will do the same for you. Of course, the greatest battle has already been won.

When Jesus died on the cross, He paid the ultimate price so we could gain unlimited favor (John 3:16). None of us deserves it. *None of us.* No matter how unbelievably fantastic our mothers tell us we are, we could never make it to heaven on our own. God has the power to rain down unlimited mercy on our lives (Ezek. 34:26), but the price was greater than any human could pay.

All we are asked to do is request forgiveness for our sins and invite Christ into our lives. Just as you protect your own family and care for their every need, God does the same (Matt. 7:11). He looks after His own.

Many people would have labeled me a cancer victim, but because of the Cross, I was a victor over cancer the very same day I was diagnosed. No matter what took place in my physical body, cancer would *never* own me. Cancer would not define me on my hardest day.

Knowing Jesus paid the ultimate price for me on the cross so many years ago, I lay down in my bed the night of my diagnosis and slept like a baby. If God is for me, who can be against me (Rom. 8:31)? This cancer diagnosis was no surprise to Him, though it left me completely breathless. God sees my end from the beginning, and no matter what my future holds, I can always trust that He keeps me in the palm of His hand (Ps. 125:1–2).

Was this easier said than done after being handed such horrific news? Yes. Of course! But what did I have to lose? According to science, I was dying, so I decided to grab onto the true source of life with both hands. Nothing would deter me from total victory through Jesus Christ. I was in it to win it.

I began to dig deeper into the Bible, looking for lessons I might have missed, trying to find that hidden golden nugget that would add even more to my experience. The wonderful thing about reading the Word is that every time you dive in, you find something new to apply to the situation you are currently facing. It is a living document that changes with our daily needs. A Bible verse that was meaningful to you during last year's financial crisis can bring a brand-new promise this year for your struggling marriage.

I love the Psalms. I could dive into this book of the Bible and really cut out the others entirely. No offense to the other prophets, but David is my kind of guy. The Bible records many heartbreaking tales throughout David's history. The part that I love most about David is that every time he royally blew it, he crawled back, completely broken, and asked God to forgive him: "Hide Your face from my sins, and blot out all my iniquities. Create in me a clean heart, O God, and renew a steadfast spirit within me. Do not cast me away from Your presence, and do not take Your Holy Spirit from me. Restore to me the joy of Your salvation, and uphold me by Your generous Spirit" (Ps. 51:9–12).

Today, when we ask God to reveal Himself to us, He is faithful to do just that. But we can't just ask Him for help. "God, I really need direction in my life for..." We have to be willing to listen. If we have already defined the answer for ourselves and are basically telling God to help us on our own terms, we are in essence telling God that we are smarter than He is and know what is best for ourselves. We are limiting God and His blessing. In so doing, we are limiting ourselves.

God wants to do things for us far greater than what we can imagine (Eph. 3:20), and with my imagination, Disney should hire me! To think that what God wants to do for me (or any of us) could far exceed the never-ending data stream flowing through my mind excites me enough to pause and realize maybe I just don't know everything after all.

Handing our super-sized problem over to God instead of

handling it ourselves does not admit weakness; it is a sign of submission. This means we are completely submitted to the will of God and are ready to receive what He deems to be in our best interest. His answers rarely match what we had in mind, but generally speaking, He takes our dime-store-budget idea and shows up with a Bentley.

THE LION OF JUDAH ROARS FOR YOU!

One of many amazing blessings that came my way after the night I spent on bended knee asking God for my complete healing was a quick ticket to MD Anderson Cancer Center in Houston, Texas, for extensive testing. I didn't know how long I would be gone, what the final determination would be, or the extent of my illness, so I expected the best and prepared for the worst.

The practical mother in me knew I had to go to my local Target and stock up on groceries and household supplies before heading out. I live in San Antonio, Texas, so it wasn't like I was headed to the North Pole, but I didn't want my kids to eat at Chick-fil-A every single day during my absence.

God bless my husband. He's a lot of great things, but a chef he is not. He can reheat with the best of them, but I wasn't sure my kids would go for endless weeks of leftovers and casseroles. Certainly leaving him alone with two young girls who would no doubt request his help with the tiniest of accessories was asking enough.

I headed to Target with my list, totally focused on buying groceries and getting back to the house post haste. There was plenty to do before leaving for Houston.

I had taken just a few small steps inside the door when a woman I didn't know approached me. "You don't know me," she began. If I had a dime for every time I heard this, I would never have to work again. In my mind I was thinking, "Just get it over with. You watch my dad on TV. You went to school with one of my siblings. I need to get ready to go to the hospital for testing. I don't have time for this. Just tell me how you know me so I can buy my groceries and get out of here." I was in full-on planning mode and wasn't in the mood for any unnecessary interruptions.

She said, "You don't know me, and I don't know you." Now she had my full attention. Either this was divine intervention or she was a complete nut case. Just in case, I was looking around to see if any security might be handy. Like it or not, the lady continued talking, "I was supposed to be at work, and I am late. My boss is going to be upset with me, but God told me to come to this store across town and walk up to the first lady I saw on my right. He said to tell her that the Lion of Judah is roaring for her, and when the Lion of Judah roars, everybody listens. I don't know what you are going through, but God has already taken care of it." And just like that she turned on her heels and walked right out the door.

There are few times in my life I have been left completely speechless. Without a doubt this was definitely one of those times.

I have to say, I completely admired her courage to walk up to a stranger and deliver a message she knew nothing about. Despite the chance that I could have laughed in her face, she obeyed God's command and delivered a message that granted me such an all-encompassing peace that no fear or negativity of any kind would be able to penetrate the hard shell of confidence that continued to surround me.

As I have said before, there is no mistaking God's presence—even in Target. You don't have to be at church for God to speak to you. You don't even have to be praying or the leader of a Bible study group. When you ask God for divine intervention, He will meet you where you are. Standing in the middle of my local Target, I was completely entrenched in the assurance that the Master had shown up to handle my impossible situation. The devil could just go straight to hell. He was not going to use this cancer diagnosis to defeat me. This was just a small bump in the road.

For if God be for me, who can be against me?

Heavenly Father,

We come before You and thank You that when bad days come our way, Your Word says not to fear. We don't have to fear the circumstances because we know that You are the Alpha and the Omega, the beginning and the end. There is nothing that happens in our lives that takes You by surprise. You have already seen our terribly bad day even before we had the faintest idea things weren't going to go our way. Though we might not have a clue about what our future holds, we know who holds tomorrow. And if Your eye is on the sparrow, we know You're watching over us. We ask that in the middle of this storm You cover us with Your wings so that no harm might come near our dwelling. May You grant us Your peace that surpasses all understanding, and may this enormous challenge that we are facing somehow bring honor and glory to Your precious name.

In Jesus's name, amen.

Chapter 2

MESSAGE IN A BOTTLE

*The Lord will fight for you; you
need only to be still.*
—EXODUS 14:14, NIV

HAVE YOU EVER seen the view from the inside of an MRI machine? The very limited view? Stuffing yourself into that machine is like placing one of those tiny pirate ships inside a bottle or like shoving a foot-long hot dog into the smallest possible bun (maybe even a dinner roll). You become a human tamale.

When I arrived at MD Anderson, I had no idea what to expect. I had a promise of healing through Psalm 61, the passage God clearly gave me right after my diagnosis. However, I had no idea how far spread my disease was or if the doctors would see any improvement during my treatment.

I had been scheduled for five weeks of radiation. Like some of you, I had no idea what that meant. Sometimes we enter life's challenges blindly, hoping to come out on the other end completely unscathed. We are at times forced to open ourselves up to new opportunities outside of our comfort zone. Radiation was definitely a new one for me, and definitely not on my bucket list.

The radiation machine is very similar to that of an MRI, in that it is enormous (think SUV size), but it glides around your body while you lie still underneath (so no worries about claustrophobia). It is also not as noisy as the MRI machine, which sounds like a golf cart backing up on steroids. The radiation machine simply sounds like a giant bug zapper. If you grew up in the South, it's a familiar summer sound and you can sleep right through it.

As I came in for my grand introduction, I was met by a radiology technician who asked if she could play a music CD she had put together especially for me. I smiled and told her I would love to hear it. I crossed my fingers hoping it would be some type of comprehensible genre. I have heard some exceptional music in my life and subscribe to almost every brand—as long as I can actually understand the words and the music doesn't sound like someone is screaming in pain or scraping together every pan in their kitchen collection. Music is an amazing gift that can take you back to a wonderful memory or elevate your spirits on the most chaotic day. And by the time I had walked through a lobby filled with people who gave a new definition to the word *sick*, I was ready for a little relaxation and to get on with my own treatment.

I lay on the radiation machine with expectations that were not very high. It had been explained to me that the treatments are lined up by a light beam and measured for accuracy in millimeters. The techs had drawn (in permanent marker) all over my right leg, marking the exact area the beam needed to penetrate, the exact location of the potentially remaining cancer cells under my skin.

As the music started to filter in, I was greeted by a welcome surprise. The message of the lyrics pouring through the loud speakers was loud and clear: "Do not be afraid. I know the situation you are in. I will be with you till the end." I had to wait until the reprise of the chorus line to make sure I had heard the words correctly. I could not believe this was the CD the tech had made for my visit. This was such a powerful message delivered out of the blue that to this day if I close my eyes, I can still hear the music playing.

I was utterly speechless. (And if you don't know me, that is saying a lot!) God had prepared a way for me in the middle of a week of absolute craziness. Just a few days earlier I had been filling out paperwork on whether or not I wanted to be revived if something went awry during testing, and now I was listening to a hope-filled message in song, another promise from God.

The treatment was over in a flash, and I asked the technician how she came about choosing that specific music for me. A sweet smile spread across her face, and I could literally feel the love of Jesus pouring out of her as she spoke. The tech who tattooed the original markings on my leg (for radiation) told her my story, and she immediately began filling a CD with songs that would minister to me from the very first radiation treatment.

Can you believe it? Here I was, just a few weeks after my cancer diagnosis, trying to find my way in a brand-new cancer-treatment sort of world, and this tech who didn't know me from the next three thousand patients she would be treating brings in a CD just for me. I was once again reminded of God's faithfulness.

No matter where we are, He will find us. No matter what we are going through, He is right beside us. You can't get any more alone than the inside of a radiation lab. But He promises, "Lo, I am with you always, even to the end of the age" (Matt. 28:20).

Every day as I began my radiation treatment, I heard the familiar clicking noise made by the sound system as the music began to fill the tiny space around me with God's presence. Each note saturated me with the peace that surpasses all understanding (Phil. 4:7). By the end of the first week other doctors who were not even associated with my treatment were coming in to tell me they were praying for my healing. If God had rented a billboard, the message could not have been any clearer.

I AM WITH YOU ALWAYS

The blessing of how deeply that tech cared for me is a constant reminder of life's small victories, but the lyrics of one special song will stay with me always. Written by Gerald Crabb and recorded by the Crabb family, "Come Down to Me" talks about how there are others more deserving that God should be helping, but because of His merciful nature, He will reach down and meet us right where we are. The moment I heard these powerful lyrics I was humbled to the core. We serve a mighty big God!

On a side note, under the "it's an incredibly small world" category, at that time I had not met the Crabbs. Today, Aaron and Amanda Crabb are the ministers of music at our church. (Aaron is Gerald Crabb's son.) Sometimes God brings us full circle just to remind us that He can.

Never would I have believed that cancer would be a part of my life, but handing that problem over to the Master showed me how to obtain one of the greatest victories of my life to date. I stopped looking at the circumstances surrounding me and started looking up to my Redeemer, the One who surrounded my circumstances. He was the One who started lining up the solutions to my problems before there was a diagnosis. And every step of the way He reminded me that He was my biggest cheerleader.

Matthew 28:20 says, "Lo, I am with you always..." This is such a powerful statement. Never will there be a time where you are looking for help from God and He's on hiatus. He is the One who sends you the perfect song in the most unexpected place. He is the One who walks you through the fire (in my case radiation) and brings you out on the other side without being consumed.

Any time I am in the middle of a storm, I stop right where I am and start pleading my case. "God, please help me with... I can't do this on my own."

As soon as the prayer leaves my lips, I know God is saying, "I will fight this battle for you. You need only to be still." (See Exodus 14:14.) And just like that, overwhelming peace begins to invade my life and I become an instant victor. Nothing has changed about my circumstances, but I have taken the debacle of the day and turned it over to the Master. I don't want to take up residence on the inside of my problem. I want to move on.

When God is coaching your team, a day that begins with "O God, what am I going to do about this?" ends with "Bring it on. I can do all things through Christ who strengthens me."

If you are currently in a small, tight spot, know that we serve a great big God who can saturate any corner of the universe with His unmistakable presence. When you are up against a wall, you will have no greater champion fighting on your side. Put on your boxing gloves and call upon His name. The ring of the bell is only the sound of sweet victory in Jesus's name.

Heavenly Father,

Your Word says that You have searched us and You know us. You are acquainted with all of our ways, not just some of them. There is nowhere we can go to escape Your love and mercy. If the darkness shall fall around us, Scripture records that with You there, the night will shine like the day. Darkness cannot hide us. We thank You that no matter how crazy life gets, You are right beside us. We are never left alone to fend for ourselves. You can find us in the tightest spot and deliver us from the greatest enemy—seen or unseen. As we put on the full armor of God, You will surely deliver us in the day of trouble. May Your mercy embrace us like the noonday sun, and may all who see us gain the victory know that the hand of God is upon us.

In Jesus's name, amen.

Chapter 3

THE GREAT PHYSICIAN

*Daughter, your faith has made you well. Go
in peace, and be healed of your affliction.*
—MARK 5:34

IN OUR MODERN society we pray for something and want God to hand deliver an answer within sixty seconds. When an answer doesn't drop from the sky in rapid succession, we start ranting in some ridiculous diatribe about how God must not love us or maybe He just isn't listening. We start anticipating the worst, waiting for the other shoe to drop. Perhaps it is *us* who need to stop and listen to *Him*. Maybe God is saving us from something worse than just a shoe dropping. If God is taking something away from us, it is because He is either saving us from ourselves (our own foolish choices), or He wants to give us something better. Yet we continue to insist that God answer our problem in the way *we* see fit.

Mark 5:25–34 tells the story of a woman who had been dealing with a particular health issue for twelve years— a long time to deal with daily discomfort. Unfortunately for this woman, she decided to take matters into her own hands. And I must admit that I completely relate to her taking this initiative. I am among the many legions of pathetically impatient human beings. I wish I had a jet so that I could avoid unnecessary traffic jams that keep me from getting to work more quickly. I wish I could just swipe my debit card at the register and not have to wait in line. I wish I could have the same assembly line afforded Jane Jetson in the cartoons, where she sits in a chair in her robe, zips through a small room with lightning speed, and comes out on the other side completely dressed with flawless hair and makeup. Where can I find one of those?

So I can understand how this woman spent all the money she had in the bank visiting doctors, desperately seeking a cure. But in the end, like so many of us, she had come to the end of her rope. Now what?

Somehow she found out that Jesus was coming to her town. She had tried everything else; why not head out and see if Jesus can help her? You can almost see her walking down the street, completely exhausted on every physical level. And as she comes into His presence, she knows that all she has to do is touch the hem of His garment to be made well.

Think about the power found in that verse. "If only I may touch His clothes, I shall be made well" (v. 28). I don't know about you, but my wardrobe doesn't function like that. On a good day it doesn't show leftovers from lunch, and on a great day it makes me look thin. But in Jesus's case, it was the power of God that literally seeped through the garment.

Jesus was walking along cobblestone streets with His disciples, wearing the traditional robe and prayer shawl (*tallit*) of a rabbi. When the woman reached out to touch the hem of His garment, she probably grabbed the ends of His prayer shawl. Woven in the ends of the shawl (what appears to be the fringe of the garment) is the name of God. As she reached out to God, she received total and instantaneous healing.

She didn't have to spend all of her time and money to receive her healing. She simply needed to reach out to God and ask for it. No co-pay required. (Think of the time and money she could have saved if she would have started with this simple act of faith.)

Jesus immediately felt that she had been healed and found her in the crowd. She was afraid, but He calmed her by saying that her faith had made her well. He doesn't say, "Take two aspirin and call Me in the morning." *Bam!* The problem was instantaneously over. Twelve years of suffering ended in the blink of an eye. *That* is my kind of healing.

LET GOD TAKE OVER

Of course, God's timing is not always our timing. Let's get real. It's almost *never* the same as our timing. We are a society screaming for instant gratification. We have drive-through hamburgers, drive-through med clinics, and drive-through divorces. There is almost nothing for which we are forced to wait.

Then, out of the blue, God will allow us to come face-to-face with a seemingly impossible challenge with no resolution in sight. We have a choice. Will we try to handle it on our own, or will we hand the problem over to God? He is desperately trying to make us into the person He knows we can be, the person created to worship and honor Him. He shows us His love in so many ways, and we sit back and say, "Hey! We don't need you. We can come up with better ideas on our own. Back off!" And so He does. And in our own foolish wisdom we remain right smack in the middle of our problem.

If we would only realize how limited and painfully short-sighted we are and allow God to work in us, the road to our divine destiny could be paved with unlimited mercy and favor. Does this mean it will be easier? Probably not. God doesn't promise to make our lives easier, but He does promise to walk beside us if we will call upon His name.

David was a great man of God who made poor choices. It makes you wonder what his life could have been like if he would have followed God's plan instead of his own desires. And I don't say this in judgment of David. I have made plenty of mistakes on my own; we all have. But God desires something so much greater for us. His Word says that our minds cannot even grasp the things He has waiting for us. His thoughts are higher than ours, and yet we continue to push Him away.

What if we stop for just a minute and allow God to take over and His will to dominate our lives? What if we admit that we are a hot mess, totally in need of a master planner? What if we start honoring God with our lives and putting His desires first when we are updating our five-year calendar?

He clearly promises to open up the windows of heaven and pour out a blessing "that there will not be room enough to receive it" (Mal. 3:10). I can't speak for you, but as far as I'm concerned, any day God wants to bless me is a very good day. Bring it!

For those of you who think this can't happen in your

own life, that it only happens to the people in the Bible or modern-day preachers, continue reading in Malachi. God literally says, "Try Me!" He says if you honor Him in your life, put Him to the test. He is the Lord, and He does not change. What He has done for others He can do for you. Put Him to the test, and you will know that He can flood you with goodness and mercy all the days of your life.

Speaking from personal experience, I will say, without hesitation or apology, that when God decides to bless you, there is no mistaking it. And there is no trading it. The peace you find on this path will encapsulate every fiber of your life, no matter the size or intensity of the storm you are facing.

I'm sure the woman with the issue of blood would completely agree with me. When the Holy Spirit fell on her, she knew in that very instance Jesus had healed her. She wasn't wondering what happened. She knew.

When you invite God into your life, there is no mistaking His presence. You feel like you can fly higher than Superman and conquer any demon with the plastic sword in your kid's toy chest. The feeling of absolute empowerment is overwhelming. This is what Romans 8:31 means when it says, "If God is for us, who can be against us?" With God on your side, you can face your greatest enemy, look him right in the eye, and say, "This is the day that the Lord has made. I will rejoice and be glad in it, because no weapon formed against me will prosper" (Ps. 118:24; Isa. 54:17).

But what happens when you doubt that God really wants to help you? When you keep calling out and feel like He isn't listening? When He isn't coming on time? When you desperately need a hand to hold but continue to try and punch your own way through life? Well, I hope you have some mighty strong gloves, because God will allow you to enjoy your problem as long as you choose to fight your own battle. Let's look at some families in the Bible that might have gone through something similar.

GOD'S TIMING IS NOT ALWAYS OUR OWN

What about Lazarus's family? When Jesus arrived at Lazarus's hometown of Bethany, Lazarus had already been in the tomb for four days. Lazarus's sister Martha asked Jesus why He hadn't come sooner. "Why could You not come in time to save my brother?" Being a sister myself, I can totally see why Martha would be upset. If Jesus was supposed to be their friend, what was the big holdup? Why wasn't He there during their greatest hour of need? On the surface it appeared that death had won.

Jesus wept at the loss of this great man, and we all know the ending to this story of absolute triumph. With just a few words Jesus commanded Lazarus to come forth from the tomb. Death had *not* won. (See Revelation 1:17–18.)

Martha and Mary learned the same lesson we sometimes hate to encounter: God's timing is not always our own. Sometimes we want things done quickly and easily so we can move on to what we perceive to be the next new and exciting event in our lives, something that holds a higher interest for us or maybe seems to hold a higher degree of importance. But God's way of thinking is higher than ours, and sometimes He uses our circumstances to teach us to call out to Him for help, to reach for the hem of His garment. (See Isaiah 55:8.)

WHAT IF...

Like Martha we often cave in to fear and doubt, even though Scripture repeatedly advises against it. Mark 5:36 says, "Do not be afraid; only believe." As humans we are constantly asking, "What if...?" My oldest daughter, Mckenzie (age eleven at the time of this conversation), is the queen of "what ifs."

One morning as I was brushing my teeth, getting ready for the workday, she came into my bathroom. "Mom, my throat hurts." Knowing that she does not like to be absent from school, I told her we had some antibiotics left over from when she had a sore throat a few weeks earlier. (Note to my wonderfully amazing pediatrician, Dr. Pauli: please do not read this section.)

"No, Mom, I hate that medicine! It tastes horrible."

"It's a pill, Mckenzie. It doesn't taste like anything. Just swallow it quickly and don't think about it."

"Trust me, Mom, it tastes bad. I will be even sicker and maybe throw up if I have to take that pill."

Fifteen minutes later we were *still* having this now-ridiculous and infuriating conversation. My polite "please take the pill" had turned into complete exhaustion. I'm not a morning person on a really good day after sleeping eight hours (which never happens) and definitely need caffeine to get me moving. I don't hit the ground running in the morning. I need a few minutes to get my motor running.

By now our pill discussion had turned into, "You can either take the pill or go to the doctor and get a shot. Or, if you like, you can do neither and just get sicker. Your choice." OK. So I wasn't up for Mom of the Year that morning. Give me a break! It wasn't even 6:00 a.m. yet! My eyelids still felt like sandpaper.

Mckenzie had given me one hundred different reasons why she didn't want to take the pill. "Will a shot hurt more than being sick from the pill? How badly will the shot hurt? Will it be a big needle? Will Dr. Pauli give me the shot in my arm, or where do you think the shot will be? Could I maybe find another medicine? What if I just skip the pill?"

I wanted to take the battery out of the Energizer Bunny and make her stop asking me questions. Take the stupid pill already! I was over this conversation that would make me run late for the start of my day...something that irritates me to no end. In my haste to get out the door, I narrowed it down to two choices: "Take the pill, or just keep the sore throat. I'm getting in the car and driving your sister to school in ten minutes, with or without you." No pills were taken. No further complaints were made about a sore throat.

As I sat behind my desk at work later that morning, I started chastising myself for not being kinder to my daughter. Yes, it was early. No, I hadn't had any caffeine. Still, it was no excuse.

I started thinking about how many times God has told me to do something and I immediately started asking Him if perhaps there was another less painful way to accomplish the same thing—my way. And, in case God hadn't thought of all the various possibilities, I quickly point out more favorable options that will ultimately take me to the same goal. I mean, don't I already have enough character?

Usually my own brilliant ideas involve a much quicker, less painful method of obtaining what I ascertain to be the most desirable outcome. Of course this route doesn't usually include much personal or spiritual growth. I mean, who wants to push themselves to become a better person when you can get what you want right away?

Without question, the times I have shut my mouth and marched up the road God planned for me (without my own addendums or detours) have yielded a far greater reward. The road wasn't necessarily shorter, quicker, or easier to travel. Sometimes it was definitely a hard, distasteful pill to swallow. But handing my problem over to Him has always brought me out to rich fulfillment (Ps. 66:10–12). If we give Him the opportunity to guide us down the road less traveled, we can come out on the other side a much richer, stronger person.

If you think Lazarus was the only one Jesus raised from the dead (in case one isn't enough for you), let me remind you of (or introduce you to) Jairus.

RULER OF THE SYNAGOGUE

The Bible calls Jairus a "ruler of the synagogue" (Mark 5:22). He clearly studied the Torah in great depth and knew that Jesus could heal his gravely ill daughter. But since he was a leader in his community, those who surrounded him were waiting to see his reaction. How would his faith take him through this challenge? Would he fall flat on his face before God or flat on his backside in total despair?

What a surprise; Jairus's schedule did not match up to Jesus's. Jairus began pleading with Jesus, telling Him that his precious daughter had a terminally high fever and without His immediate attention she would surely die. Mark 5:22–23 describes the scene like this: "And when he [Jairus] saw Him [Jesus], he fell at His feet and begged Him earnestly, saying, 'My little daughter lies at the point of death. Come and lay Your hands on her, that she may be healed, and she will live.'"

If you have been a parent long enough for your child to become sick just one time, you know there is no feeling more helpless than a small sick child whom you cannot cure. Just watching a child with a fever is horrible. Knowing your child could die from the fever would spur any parent to action. When your child needs something, especially something that so clearly affects the quality of their life, there are no limits to what a parent will do.

Jairus fell at the feet of Jesus and begged for His help. Even as the words were tumbling out of his mouth, the members of Jairus's community came to tell him that his daughter was already dead. "There is no reason to bother the Master, Jairus. Clearly He is too late to help you." With encouraging friends like that, it would almost make you want to quit the synagogue!

And yet, in the middle of this whirlwind of emotion and chaos, Jesus remained completely calm. He told Jairus, "Do not be afraid; only believe" (v. 36). Right about here I have to admit I would be in full-on panic mode. As a mother I would be reiterating for Jesus one more time: "Jesus! What do You mean? My daughter is dead! This is not the time to tell me not to be afraid. Is there anything You can do to fix it? Please help me!"

But Jairus, still dripping with the pain inflicted by the words announcing his daughter's death, obeyed Jesus and simply followed Him back to his house. He did not question Jesus or offer Him worthless words of advice. He simply turned and followed Jesus back to his house. You can only imagine that with every excruciating footstep Jairus was coming to the realization that his precious daughter was gone forever. Never again would he get to hold her chubby hand or watch her tiny curls blow in the breeze. Her life was *over*.

Arriving at home, Jairus encountered another group of encouraging synagogue congregants, loudly mourning the death of his daughter. There were people standing in his yard and filtering in and out of his house. It was clear that Jesus had arrived too late. Still Jairus did not doubt Jesus, did not question the hour of His late arrival. When everything around him was screaming, "Just give up," Jairus continued to trust God.

Jesus entered the house and said, "Why make this commotion and weep? The child is not dead, but sleeping" (Mark 5:39). And the people began to mock Jesus. (This part of the story kind of makes you not feel so bad about the naysayers in your own crowd or the snakes in your garden.)

Jesus asked the mourners to leave the house, and He headed straight for the girl's bedroom with the parents, Peter, James, and John. (Notice He placed all the doubters outside the equation and left those who had faith inside to witness one of the great miracles of the Bible.)

Jesus simply said, "Little girl, I say to you, arise" (v. 41). And because of the faith of her parents and because her father sought the Master in his greatest hour of need and never questioned Him (even when it looked like the circumstances were terminal), the little girl arose, and they all had dinner together. Can you imagine the celebration going on at that dinner table? While the people on the front lawn were mourning a little girl's death and planning her funeral, the parents were inside having dinner with her! Pass the falafel please.

God Is in Control—Don't Worry About a Thing

There are so many lessons in this story, but let's concentrate on just a few. First, and most importantly, if God is in control, you don't need to worry about a thing. He will arrive right on time.

Don't worry about the overly encouraging people around you saying that your miracle will never happen, your daughter is dead, your dream is dead, or your marriage is dead. Don't listen to them when they say, "Don't bother God with your needs; there's no chance of ever realizing your goals." The Bible says to place your "hope in God" (Ps. 42:11).

When God says something is going to happen, you need to take your tiny mustard seed of faith and get ready for amazing things to start happening. Don't look at the circumstances that surround you. Look at the One who surrounds your circumstances. Don't listen to the crowd planning your demise; listen to the One who commands the winds and waves to be still with just three words: "Peace, be still" (Mark 4:39).

If you are looking for a way out of a hopeless situation, look to the way maker. If God can part the Red Sea and allow the Israelites to march right through the middle with all of their earthly belongings and in the next breath swallow up every last enemy, He can help drown the enemies in your life. *Nothing* is too big for God.

Trusting God is a lifelong process. And I don't say this tritely or because I read that it works really well in a wonderful, self-help book somewhere. I have seen God carve holes through the center of insurmountable mountains in my own life.

We serve an awesome and all-powerful God! And when you call upon His name in the day of trouble, He is faithful to show up right on time (Ps. 50:15).

Heavenly Father,

As we face overwhelming health issues, may You be our first thought and not our last hope. May we truly come to understand what it means to touch the hem of Your garment, to seek first the kingdom of God. With You we have total and complete healing in our lives, in our health, in our homes, in our finances, in our marriages. There is no area of our being that You cannot touch and bring back to life. Father God, the area that we most need Your healing touch in our lives is _____. We ask that You remove all fear and doubt. Satan can use this as a tool against us, and we invite You to step in as Lord and Master, controlling every part of our being. We thank You for healing us, for You alone are the great physician. We give You all praise, honor, and glory for the good things that are on the way.

In Jesus's name, amen.

Chapter 4

A LIMITLESS LIFE

Ask, and you will receive, that your joy may be full.
—JOHN 16:24

IF YOU SURVIVE the first five years of sarcoma treatment, your chances of living will drastically increase to 20 percent."

These were the words still buzzing in my head when, during year two of my recovery from leiomyosarcoma, I was told that my thyroid had to be removed because of the possibility of a second and completely unrelated cancer. By this time I had heard the "C" word connected to my name so many times that the ripple effect was like the very last wave in a pond before you can hardly tell a pebble even struck the water's surface. The shock and awe phase was over, and I was ready to meet with a different set of doctors and set up a new plan of attack. I was not going to let anyone steal my joy.

What did we learn in our high school science class from our good friend Isaac Newton? The Law of Motion says, "To every action there is always an equal and opposite reaction."

In my life this has always been the wave of negativity and naysayers who are self-appointed balloon poppers. You know who they are—the ones who are constantly telling you why something good can't possibly last, waiting for the comforting cloud that is protecting you from the noonday sun to suddenly start pelting you relentlessly with hail. These are the precious souls who remind you of the bad things that have happened in your life, and thoroughly enjoy rehearsing all things negative. They are the Eeyore to your Winnie the Pooh.

God bless them all. They are a real pain!

But they are right about some things. They will not be happy for you because they are not happy with themselves. The Bible says not to let anyone steal your joy or your peace. John 15:11 says, "These things have I spoken to you, that My joy remain in you, and that your joy may be full."

There is never a bad time in your life to just stop what you are doing and saturate yourself with the joy of the Lord. Joy is different from happiness. Happiness is based upon circumstances. Joy is based upon a relationship with Jesus Christ, regardless of your circumstances. If I waited for the stars to align and everything in my life to be perfect, I would be happy about 2 percent of the time...maybe less. But true joy is a gift from God, and no man (or circumstance) can take it from you.

If someone you know is constantly negative, never finding a morsel of goodness in any of life's special moments, they are clearly not filled with the spirit of joy. (Understatement of the century, right?) The truth of the matter is that no one can take anything away from you that you don't hand over—willingly or unwillingly. They can't take your peace, and you can't give them yours. Since God grants true peace, it isn't yours to give (2 John 3). As much as you would like to share your peace with them, this is a gift from God straight to you. They will have to ask for their own.

To those who want to continue sucking on life's lemons and living life to the *un*fullest, I say, "Go for it!" Just don't expect those around you who love and appreciate life to sit around and listen to you spewing unkindness. Bad things happen to every breathing person. You are not the only one to ever face a difficult moment.

Forgiveness Helps Us Maintain the Joy of the Lord

Hard times are for self-improvement, for building a relationship with God, and for moving on. If you feel the need to rehearse someone else's failures or shortcomings, telling them how undeserving they are, perhaps you need to look in the mirror. The Bible says we have *all* sinned and fallen short of the glory of the Lord (Isa. 53:6; Rom. 3:23). No one needs a full-time micromanager hanging around to remind them of past failures. Our job is never to judge someone else. That is God's job, so leave it to Him and worry about your own shortcomings.

For our sins we ask forgiveness, and then we move on. No rehearsal necessary. One of the many beauties of the Cross is if we ask forgiveness, that's it (Eph. 1:7). Our sin is gone, forgotten, and never to be remembered again.

As a small public service, may I remind you that the Bible clearly says we aren't to rehearse the bad that others have done to us either. We are to forgive them and move on as if nothing ever happened, not keep a tally sheet of all offenses. We treat our neighbors just as we would want them to treat us (Luke 6:31), with dignity, respect, and a healthy dose of forgiveness.

When we forgive others, this releases us from carrying around useless grievances. It also allows God to forgive us. (See Matthew 6:14–15.) Certainly there is no one alive today who doesn't need God's forgiveness. So, as we obey His command to forgive others, we are released from that burden of anger and bitterness. We are no longer mastered by the events that led us to harsh words or ungodly circumstances.

Forgiveness is one of the biggest blessings I can think of, and it's one that can grant us eternal life. Is this something you're willing to give up because your least favorite relative forgot to invite you to their Christmas party last year? Get over it!

You *can* live life without limit. Don't limit yourself, and don't allow others to limit you by harboring anger in your soul. Uncontrolled anger can drive you to a place of total destruction and despair. Life is too short and the power of love is too great to allow a few events in the course of a lifetime to shape your entire future. I have heard my dad say a million times, "It is better to be reconciled than to be right."

HOLD ON TO YOUR JOY!

Sometimes negativity smacks us in the face, completely taking us by surprise. This has happened to me personally on several occasions, and I'm sure to you as well. When the doctor told me I might also have thyroid cancer, I was 100 percent unconcerned. I would have worried more about finding a parking space at the mall during the Christmas shopping season. I had already been healed of an aggressive cancer and knew that if anything came of this tiny thyroid issue, it would be a no-brainer for God. He already had this covered before my doctor delivered the news.

This is why I was so shocked when the naysayers kicked into full gear immediately after hearing I *might* have another cancer. One flapping jaw at a time, the negativity began to seep in. "I'm sure you must have done something to make this happen. People don't normally get cancer, and you might have two now."

I just continued to smile, which makes someone totally crazy who is trying to get under your skin. Like most every other cancer patient in the universe, I have read the statistics from the American Cancer Society's website. I rejoice every time I look down the columns listing every type of cancer currently charted by hospitals. Having been diagnosed with one of the rarest forms, I know that every day I am given breath I am a living miracle, beating every possible human odd.

So yes, I smile. All the time.

I was even smiling as I limped slowly, painfully through the pedestrian walkway into my neighborhood Target, still recovering from my last surgery. I had just been allowed to start driving again when a self-righteous patron came fuming around the corner in his beat-up pick-up truck. As he screamed at me, a crowd started to gather in front of the store. "Hey, you! Why are you parked in that handicapped parking space? There's nothing wrong with you! Get out of that space! I'm calling security."

I have to say that my first thought was not to share the love of the Lord with him. I wanted to punch him right in the face and show him the hundreds of stitches literally holding my leg together, neatly interlaced from top to bottom in a life-saving and yet horrific pattern. But I took a really deep breath (or maybe ten) and turned toward his truck with my best fake smile. "Thank you so much for your concern, sir. You see, recently I had my entire leg reconstructed after they removed a rare and aggressive cancer that should have killed me. By God's grace I'm still here. And now I'm trying to regain the use of my leg by walking short distances. I would be happy to roll up my pants and show you the scars if you'd like." He could not get out of that parking lot fast enough.

I was not letting *anyone* steal my joy (John 14:27).

For those who think you have to do something horrible to get cancer, let me share something with you. (And yes, I know that smoking *may* lead to lung cancer. Overexposure to the sun *may* lead to skin cancer. Blah. Blah.) Ask any oncologist; not *every* cancer has a direct causal link. Sometimes cancer happens.

According to the American Cancer Society, in 2010 over 1.5 million people were diagnosed with cancer. Over 569,000 people died that same year.[*] Were all of these people horribly sinful so God decided to strike them with a lightning bolt of cancer? I don't think so.

The Bible says that vengeance belongs to the Lord (Heb. 10:30), but He is not sitting on an enormous throne like Zeus, throwing down lightning bolts of punishment: "Didn't say your prayers before work this morning." Zap! "Didn't go to Bible study last Thursday night." Zap! "Didn't

---

[*] American Cancer Society, *Cancer Facts and Figures 2010* (Atlanta: American Cancer Society, 2010), http://www.cancer.org/acs/groups/content/@epidemiology-surveilance/documents/document/acspc-026238.pdf (accessed February 27, 2013).

read the story of David and Goliath to your kids at bedtime last night." Zap!

TRUSTING IN GOD LEADS TO A LIMITLESS LIFE

If you still don't think this whole trusting in God thing is for you, let me remind you (or inform you) of a few people in the Bible who called upon the name of the Lord in their day of trouble and things turned out OK.

Have you heard of Daniel and his hungry friends in the lion's den? Daniel could have easily been a quick afternoon snack. But God intervened on his behalf. What about his friends Shadrach, Meshach, and Abednego? God showed up Himself in the fiery furnace. He didn't send His union rep or an angel who wasn't otherwise occupied; He showed up Himself. The Bible says that not one hair on their heads was burned. I would say that qualifies as divine assistance.

Let's delve into the story of Shadrach, Meshach, and Abednego just a bit. We have probably all read the children's story with the fancy illustrations of flames pouring off of each page, brightly painted in every possible shade of red and orange. But have you really looked at the meanings buried within the story and the miraculous things God did for them? He can do these very same things for us today when we find ourselves in the middle of our own fiery trial.

These three young men were initially summoned by King Nebuchadnezzar after hearing they would not bow to him or serve the gods he had placed in authority. Statues had been erected throughout the land, and these were the gods that were to be exalted, according to the king, under penalty of death.

Shadrach, Meshach, and Abednego weren't having any of it! They made an unprecedented, bold stand against the king, proclaiming they would *only* serve the God of Israel. This outraged Nebuchadnezzar, so he sent for the three amigos. Once they arrived, the king made it very clear: "If you do not worship, you shall be cast immediately into the midst of a burning fiery furnace." And then he taunted them with, "And who is the god who will deliver you from my hands?" (Dan. 3:15).

Daniel 3:16–18 is the most telling part of the story for me. It is a blatant statement of unwavering faith. "Shadrach, Meshach, and Abed-nego answered and said to the king, 'O Nebuchadnezzar, we have no need to answer you in this matter. If that is the case, our God whom we serve is able to deliver us from the burning fiery furnace, and He will deliver us from your hand, O king. But if not, let it be known to you, O king, that we do not serve your gods, nor will we worship the gold image which you have set up.'"

These three were placed in an impossible situation. They defied the king without apology, clearly stating they would obey God's commandment to not have any other gods before Him. This sounds pretty easy, but you need to realize that during this time period there were severe consequences, most of which resulted in death. They didn't just kick you out of the church or print your picture in the paper as a lead protestor. They burned you alive, stoned you, or found some other method to end your life as slowly and painfully as possible.

And yet, even as they were summoned to the palace, these three Hebrew boys stood firm. "We will not serve you. We will not bow down." Hats off. I think it's pretty gutsy to stand in front of the most powerful man in the world and say, "No!" They were not going to give up on their core values for the sake of convenience, even if refusal meant death.

This blatant disobedience outraged King Nebuchadnezzar even further, and he immediately ordered his guards to increase the heat of the flames to seven times its normal temperature. He then ordered his guards to tie the hands of the three Hebrew boys so they could not escape the flames. (You have to wonder about this king. Did he think the ropes they were tied with could withstand the flames and keep them in place?)

And even as Shadrach, Meshach, and Abednego faced a most certain and excruciating death, they looked the king right in the eye and said, "God will deliver us...but if not..." They were saying that *no matter what*, they were going to serve the God of Abraham, Isaac, and Jacob. If it cost them their lives, they weren't going to bow to the king or pray to graven images.

Sometimes we think God isn't listening because He doesn't work within our timetable or exactly how we would have Him to function. We want X and He gives us Y. And when X isn't delivered in thirty seconds, we start feeling sorry for ourselves and doubting God.

But here are three young boys getting ready to be burned alive and watch the flesh literally melt off their bones. Instead of throwing a pity party, they defiantly look right into the king's face and say, "We will *not* serve you. Even if God does not deliver us from this fire, we will *never* bow to you." They didn't throw their hands in the air and give up just because they couldn't pinpoint the outcome. Even though the immediate future didn't hold much promise, they didn't bend to peer pressure. They stood up for what they knew to be the righteous choice without wavering and without apology.

Psalm 107:2 says, "Let the redeemed of the LORD say so, whom He has redeemed from the hand of the enemy." They were saying it loud and proud. And what happened? When they headed toward the fiery pit, the guards who pushed them in were burned alive. But God showed up and protected Shadrach, Meshach, and Abednego. He was the fourth man in their fire and caused not one hair on their heads to be singed. On their way out, they didn't even smell like smoke.

Because of this great demonstration, the king was convinced there was only one true God. Because of the faithfulness and perseverance of three young Hebrew boys, a nation turned back to serving the Lord (Dan. 3:25–29).

WELCOME TO THE JUNGLE

Some of you might be thinking, "What does this really have to do with me, with my life today? These are just old Bible stories from years ago." The Bible says that God "is the same yesterday, today, and forever" (Heb. 13:8). This means that the very same God of Israel who showed up for Daniel, Shadrach, Meshach, and Abednego so many years ago can and will show up for you today.

You don't feel like you are facing the hungry lions? How is your job going? Is the executive board about to vote you off the island due to budget cuts? How is your marriage? Are your children following God's plan for their lives? Now you get the picture. Welcome to the jungle, my friend. How is your faith going to take you through the dilemma you are currently facing?

Faith is not a feeling. Faith is what we call in elementary school an "action word." We have faith and God takes action. It doesn't take much on our parts to have faith in a God who never fails. And yet we consistently question His methods and responses. What would happen if we just stopped with the questions and started saying "Thank You for the answer that is already on the way" each time we face a new challenge.

Let me introduce my friend (and neighbor) Darren to you. Darren is a great guy, loves the Lord, attends church regularly, and even hosts a weekly Bible study in his home. His children go to a private Christian school and his wife works for a local church. His life couldn't possibly scream CHRISTIAN any more than it already does.

The point I'm making is that bad things happen to God's people. No one is able to completely avoid conflict or pain. Even though Darren had been a committed employee for more than thirteen years, his company decided (like so many others) to downsize during a rough patch in the economy. Surely they would keep him on. He had been so faithful to his job. And yet the notice arrived. Within a few weeks Darren's job would no longer exist.

His wife e-mailed and asked that we start praying for their family, that God would intervene and send the right job Darren's way. I told her I would start praying immediately, expecting God's very best. Knowing that downsizing is a horribly difficult part of life that has affected so many of us across the globe, I started specifically praying for peace in the middle of the storm. With more people on the unemployment line every day, surely looking for a new job would be a daunting task.

Dear God,

You see Darren's dilemma. You know the spot that he is in. You knew that he was going to be here facing this giant before his company even knew their plan to downsize. The enemy comes to rob, to kill, and to destroy. I ask that You give Darren wisdom and favor. That what You have for his latter days will be greater than his former. We bind the enemy from the plans he might have for Darren's family and thank You for the divine blessing that is already on the way. We know that all good and perfect gifts come from above, and we are asking You to drop a gift in his lap that could only come from You. When this gift comes, all around will only be able to say that truly the Lord did this, truly His hand was upon this family. We give You all the praise, honor, and glory.

In Jesus's name, amen.

The longer I prayed, the more I felt surrounded by an enormous cloud of total peace. I just knew without a shadow of a doubt that this family would be fine, that God had already orchestrated the perfect plan to give them a bright financial future. I didn't know how this plan was going to unfold or when, but I knew that God was looking down on them and saying, "Have faith in Me. I see you, and I will supply all of your needs according to *My* riches, not according to what the world says or wants to give you, but according to the riches that I have at My unlimited disposal." They had been faithful servants, and God would not forsake them.

I e-mailed Darren's wife and told her I felt completely at peace. (I'm sure she was thinking, "Of course you do! You aren't the one whose job is on the line.") I explained that I felt in my spirit that God was telling them to just have faith and that He would move the mountains necessary to secure their future. I knew that the answer was on the way; I just wasn't sure where it was coming from. Sometimes God wants to see how we will react to a situation. Will we follow His commands (like Shadrach, Meshach, and Abednego), or will we try to figure out our own plan and remain stuck in a problem we cannot solve? I encouraged her to be still and listen to what God was trying to tell them during this time.

The days and weeks ticked slowly by, and yet they were being propelled at lightning speed toward the final day of Darren's employment. What were they going to do? They continued e-mailing their circle of Bible-believing friends, asking everyone to lift them up in prayer, asking for divine intervention. There were only two weeks until they were left with only one income.

Darren continued to do his part, not wasting time on self-pity. While finishing up the duties required of his current position, he began interviewing with his current company as well as outside companies. With each interview came another wave of rejection, another reason why he wasn't the perfect candidate. And the prayers continued.

With less than one week left of employment, Darren received a completely unexpected call. It was not another response telling him that the job he applied for had been filled. It was the HR department of his current company saying that a manager had seen his résumé and wanted to hire him. This was a position for which Darren had not even applied, something of which he was completely unaware.

God had orchestrated the perfect job to literally land in his lap. Darren did his part (looking for a new job while giving his current job his very best, trusting that God would send an answer in due time), and God did His part. The combined efforts were sheer perfection. Darren would not go one day without pay, lose one hour of earned vacation time, or have a lapse in benefits. He would continue on in his new position as if his old one had never ended.

How amazing is God? When you hear something like this, I don't understand how anyone can doubt that God is completely in control and wants us to have unlimited blessings when we trust Him to guide us in His will.

As human beings we often focus on the problem and not the solution. We get lost in the maze instead of looking for a way out. We start to sink in the mire of questions and self-propelled doubt. So many of us have been taught to have a stiff upper lip and soldier on through our problems, but God's Word says that He is ready, willing, and able to help at any time. It's OK to admit we are weak human beings and totally in need of a Savior.

If you have a problem, congratulations! It means you are still breathing. Be thankful for the problem, ask for help, and believe that God will show up in His perfect timing and absolutely take your breath away (John 14:13). Think of Darren. When it looked like his job was over with absolutely nothing on the horizon, God came in with just a few days to spare and handed him an even better position than the one he lost. This was a brand-new source of income handed to him on a silver platter. Why? Darren trusted God with his problem and his family was saved.

Sometimes we might be persuaded that problems mean God doesn't love us or that we don't have favor with God. This is just the enemy trying to convince us that we are not good enough for God's love. Nothing could be further from the truth. For God so loved the world that He gave His ONLY Son just for you (John 3:16), even if you were the only one on the planet.

God doesn't ask where you have come from; He already knows. He wants to provide for your future and bring you into rich fulfillment. Don't linger in self-doubt any longer; instead let Him heal whatever is broken, and embrace the limitless life God has for you.

Heavenly Father,

May Your Spirit fill us with Your glory and joy unspeakable. May we come to know You in a very real and true way, as the guiding light for our lives. For where there is light, darkness must flee. May Your light shine through us, like a beacon of truth for others seeking help. We have been settling for survival mode, struggling through a life of our own making. We ask You to please forgive us for making foolish choices that have led us down a weary and painful path. We know this is not the abundant life You planned for us, and we ask You to please help us begin anew today. We want to serve You above all others. We want to trust You in good times and bad, with money in the bank and when we're flat broke. If we are feeling the fiery flames of life licking our heels, let us not give in to temptation or take the easy way out, but let us follow the commands found in Your Word so that we might obtain the rich fulfillment You have promised.

In Jesus's name, amen.

Chapter 5

THROUGH THE FIRE

Oh, bless our God, you peoples! And make the
voice of His praise to be heard, who keeps our
soul among the living, and does not allow our
feet to be moved. For You, O God, have tested
us; You have refined us as silver is refined. You
brought us into the net; You laid affliction on
our backs. You have caused men to ride over our
heads; we went through fire and through water;
but You brought us out to rich fulfillment.

—PSALM 66:8–12

IN DECEMBER OF 2008 my thyroid was removed due to the possibility of a second cancer, noting that there were "too many tumors to count." The surgery sounded pretty easy to me after having spent so much time in the operating room reconstructing my leg. A three-hour surgery was like a commercial break compared to what my body had endured in recent years.

I wasn't concerned in the least. God had my back. I was relatively sure I could have performed this easy peasy surgery myself. Have you seen the commercial where the guy is propped up at his kitchen table with his telephone on speaker? "Where do I cut?" he asks, kitchen knife in hand, as the nurse explains the exact location on his rib cage.

Coming home with just a few inches of teal blue sutures in my neck, I barely looked like I had an excuse to be in the hospital. My voice was out for a few days (which probably made my husband's week), but forty-eight hours later it was business as usual. I was ready to go back to work, get on with the mountain of laundry that had accumulated during my short hospital stint, and even tackle grocery shopping. I felt great! Look out, world; here I come!

The hard part came after the surgery, when I found out exactly how much the thyroid does to make my body function correctly. I was so out of whack, I didn't know which way was up. I felt like a cornucopia of discomfort with misery spilling out everywhere. The joy was literally being sucked right out of me.

Up was down. Hot was cold. Day was night. I couldn't sleep. I wasn't hungry. I couldn't get warm at night or cool off during the day. Why in the world was I so miserable when every one of my cancer markers was clean? Didn't this mean I was well and ready to move on with my life?

I was about to turn forty, so I understood that certain changes were going to be taking place in my body, but I wasn't ready to check into the retirement center just yet. I wasn't ready for my body to slip into crazy mode. However, if these were the changes, then I wanted to find a good plastic surgeon and turn back time (with Cher).

But how do you give your hormones a face-lift? I began to suffer from unrelenting depression because the prescribed medication was totally off the charts (unbeknownst to me).

I desperately needed the joy in my life not only to be

restored but also to be poured out upon me like never before. I wanted overwhelming joy to come like a cleansing flood. I wanted it to wash away the cobwebs forming in my brain so that I could regain a clear focus on what was important in my life.

I didn't want to be tired all the time, unable to conquer the smallest functions after dinner. By 3:00 p.m. my body was finished for the day! Dinner was an excruciating task. I wanted to walk in the sunshine and enjoy the abundant life God had given me a second chance to live. Clearly, since He had healed me from cancer, He was not finished with my story...and He did not intend for me to live in agony.

This particular piece of my journey was like walking down a long, dusty road in thin, plastic flip-flops with the sun blazing down in my face, relentless with no end in sight.

For someone suffering from a physical depression due to a medical situation, this is a debilitating reality—not a choice. You almost feel as if you are a prisoner in your own body, with no way out. You are trapped in a solitary confinement without walls.

Different types of pain leaked from every pore in my body. My head hurt because I was exhausted from unrelenting insomnia. I wasn't hungry, and yet I was constantly gaining weight. At night my body temperature dropped so low that I would often sleep in a coat with blankets piled on top. Some nights I would stack my cats on top of me to share body heat. I'm sure I looked like the crazy cat lady you see on the late night news or those hoarding shows, but I felt so miserable that I just didn't care. I desperately craved an escape from this nightmare.

In the morning I wanted to dress for work in a tube top

or a bikini because I felt like my body temperature was that of a raging volcano in full eruption mode. (I'm not sure my coworkers would have appreciated this, but you get the picture.) My joints ached. My blood pressure was up, and my energy level was down. Every time someone sneezed near me, I caught their cold. My immune system was nonexistent.

My emotions were like a runaway train. One minute everything was great, and then my daughter would tell me she didn't know her homework assignment. The tiniest things would make me feel completely out of control. My heart would start pounding as if my chest was going to burst while I was sitting on the couch watching TV. How's that for a resting heart rate?

It was as if I was in a very dark room and could see a sliver of light coming through a tiny window on the door. My fingers kept brushing up against the door, but I couldn't turn the knob. I couldn't get out of this deep, dark well that I kept sinking into as if surrounded by quicksand. The darkness was unforgiving.

My cancer treatments were a breeze compared to dealing with my entire body being thrown into complete upheaval. I had completely lost myself, and I had no idea how to come back.

I had no doubt that God would pull me through this horrific nightmare and save me from this unbearable weight that applied stress to every area of my life. My body was suffering a complete hormonal breakdown and all systems were not go, Houston.

NO CHOCOLATE FILLING HERE

I don't care if *stressed* is *desserts* spelled backward. There is no chocolate filling or wonderful icing to take the edge off of uncontrollable physical stress. When your body is revolting, whether you want to admit it out loud or not, you become emotionally stressed. No one likes to talk about the downside or aftereffects of what intense medical treatments can do to you, but they are very real.

I'm not afraid to say that my life was completely turned upside down by depression, and more people were ready to judge me than help me. I talk openly about this not because I'm so proud of this stage of my life, but to let those who are suffering through depression know they are not alone.

Some people will tell you that you aren't spiritual enough if you are facing something like depression. They think that maybe you don't trust God enough. Maybe God isn't listening to your prayers. Surely He has forgotten someone who has so many problems they can't conquer with a stiff upper lip. I can tell you that anyone saying something this ridiculous is completely ignorant. No one has ever conquered anything by denying that it exists. Stuffing a problem down a black hole of emotions and pretending everything is fine is not a solution. Get a grip!

Hold your head up high and know that there is a loving God who would love nothing more than to help get your life back on track. The Bible says that He will never leave us or forsake us (Heb. 13:5) and that He is the friend who sticks closer than any brother (Prov. 18:24). It also says that He is familiar with our struggles (Heb. 4:15) and that He was a "Man of sorrows and acquainted with grief" (Isa. 53:3). Every place you hurt, He has hurt.

Just because you have a problem does not mean that you are weak or any less spiritual. It doesn't mean that God has forgotten about you...even for one millisecond. A problem is God's way of gift-wrapping an amazing opportunity of blessing. If you have fallen, His greatest delight is leaning down to lend you a helping hand.

If you have never been stressed in your life and have no idea what I'm talking about, then more power to you. However, at this point in my life I was über stressed. I started to feel like the creature from the Black Lagoon, like someone who just wanted to sink into the deep water and be left alone. At the same time I was someone who desperately wanted to feel better. I continued to pray without ceasing that God would once again completely transform my life with an enormous joy infusion.

Stress isn't good for cancer patients. I love it when people tell me this, when in fact I *can* come in out of the rain all by myself now. This statement implies that stress is good for most other people, just not cancer patients. And if you have ever been a cancer patient (or a patient in the hospital for more than five minutes in a row), you know that a certain measure of stress is just part of the game plan. It's the breath caught in your lungs as you wait for lab results. It's the high blood pressure reading before you go in to meet with your doctor. It's the waiting in between MRIs to see if there is any new growth around your initial tumor site. It's wondering if the blood results will come back clean.

The part that stumped me the most was how a thyroid surgery could be so much more difficult than cancer. If anyone would have told me this golden nugget of truth in 2006 when I was having my leg reconstructed, I would have laughed in their face. At that point I was wondering if anything could be more challenging than a massive cancer surgery with two small children at home while trying to keep my job and not lose my insurance. I would find out that was just the prologue, a veritable appetizer in the seven-course meal that was on the way. It was the opening act to the never-ending play that had landed me in a very macabre scene.

BUT GOD!

One night I was relatively sure I was turning into the crazy cat lady, so I got down on my knees and asked God to please help me. Yes, I had asked before, but at this point I felt like I would crack in half if God didn't intervene on my behalf. I needed Him to reach down to me and tell me everything was going to be OK. Since most people don't really want to listen or spend quality time as you struggle through depression, I knew there was one place I could turn for help.

Dear God,

I know that once again You have given me this challenge for a reason. I don't know why, and I can't say I'm particularly fond of this one. But if You could please make my path straight, if only for a little while . . . if You could reveal the unknown to me . . . if You could please let me know how I can get out from under this horrible fog, I will be forever grateful. I'm of no use to my children this way. I'm of no use to my husband. I'm of no use to anyone. Please bring me back to the joy of my salvation.

Thank You for the answer that is already on the way.

And Satan, I speak to you in Jesus's name. You can take this depression and stick it where the Son doesn't shine. I will no longer accept this as a way of life. I was created to live life more abundantly, and you cannot take that away from me. You will not steal my joy. You will not steal my peace. I'm telling you to back off right now, because I will praise the God of Abraham, Isaac, and Jacob until the day I no longer have air in my lungs. And then I will start praising Him for real.

O God, I praise You, and I worship You. I give You praise for both the good and the bad that comes my way. For in You I find my strength. In You I find my peace. I can do all things through You, and I can't do anything without You. I ask that You give me strength for this journey and make me an overcomer in all areas of my life. Please take this depression from me.

Amen.

No, I did not wake up in the morning with Mr. Bluebird on my shoulder (Uncle Remus), but things dramatically changed for me very quickly after that. It had been almost a full year that I had been combating the effects of too much medication. I had been prescribed enough medication for someone twice my size (which is perhaps why I was turning into someone twice my size, one Fig Newton at a time). My body simply could not process the drugs running through my system, and it was like a computer system that had a destructive virus. Everything was short-circuiting my mainframe.

Within days of this prayer a new doctor was recommended to me, who was immediately able to pinpoint the problem (too much medication). I continued to pray without ceasing. I didn't want to continue this downward spiral of incessant gloom, knowing that a body takes months to acclimate to new medication levels. I didn't want to make a career out of visiting doctors and feeling like my skin was on fire.

I wasn't going to allow even the smallest opening for Satan in my life, no room for a seed of doubt that my body might never return to a state of normalcy. I didn't want him telling me what I couldn't do, that I wasn't good enough, or that I didn't deserve another healing.

I knew where I wanted to be. I was just having trouble getting there at the speed I wanted to travel. I wanted to click the button on the elevator an extra twenty times and get to the next level right away. I wasn't crazy about waiting for another answer. But I also knew in my spirit that God was working in me (even through all of this craziness), and so I did what I always do when I have no idea where to turn. I opened my Bible and started reading the promises found in God's Word. I started in the Psalms and worked my way through too many promises to count, until my eyes were burning. If my doctors were going to tell me there were too many tumors to count, I was going to form a counter-defensive attack and read so many promises in God's Word that it made the devil's head spin. I wanted Satan to know that he could not control my spiritual life no matter how hard he tried, no matter what brand of crazy he threw my way. I was putting on the whole armor of God and coating my world with scriptures so that no room existed for doubt, fear, or discouragement (Eph. 6:10–18).

Philippians 1:6 says, "Being confident of this very thing, that he which hath begun a good work in you will perform it until the day of Jesus Christ" (KJV).

Psalm 34:19 says, "Many are the afflictions of the righteous: but the LORD delivereth him out of them all" (KJV).

The doctors had given me bits of hope here and there, but generally speaking the news was a grim picture focusing on what I might never be able to do again. But God. What an amazing thing to be able to smile in the face of adversity and say, "Greater is he that is in [me], than he that is in the world" (1 John 4:4, KJV). No diagnosis can take the promises of God's Word away from you. No diagnosis.

Slowly the veil of depression began to lift as I continued to seek God's face for my total healing. I also continued to see the new doctor who had discovered the miscalculation of my medication. It wasn't easy, and it certainly wasn't fast (much to my chagrin), but God gave me a whole new appreciation for a healthy lifestyle.

One Friday evening I started counting my blessings again, thinking back to what some of my original doctors had said and how God's mercy had proven so many of them wrong. So, in homage to another doctor whose bad news never came to fruition, I sat in my front yard and sang my heart out, loud and proud. I threw corn out for the deer and sang every song I could think of with the words "thank you" or "hallelujah" in it. That night I had a concert to praise God for His goodness with fifty deer and one thousand angels in attendance (Ps. 68:4). Fortunately my neighbors didn't complain or call the cops.

Why would I sit in the front yard and praise the Lord? If you flip through almost any chapter in the Psalms, you will find that we are commanded to praise the Lord in good times and bad. When things don't go our way, we are to thank Him for the challenge and thank Him for the answer that is on the way. When things go well, we are to thank Him for the victory.

The Bible says, "Let everything that has breath praise the LORD" (Ps. 150:6). If we start to read through the Psalms, we come across verses like these:

> Bless the LORD, O my soul;
> And all that is within me, bless His holy name!
> Bless the LORD, O my soul,
> And forget not all His benefits:
> Who forgives all your iniquities,
> Who heals all your diseases,
> Who redeems your life from destruction,
> Who crowns you with lovingkindness and tender
>   mercies,
> Who satisfies your mouth with good things,
> So that your youth is renewed like the eagle's.
> —PSALM 103:1–5

And that is just the first five verses of the chapter! When we praise God for what He has done, we are releasing the Holy Spirit to work in our lives, to flood us with joy unspeakable and peace that no man can take away. We are telling God that we have surrendered to His will. We are looking for our kingdom purpose and not a way of life that is easy or convenient, something that grants us fleeting happiness. We are seeking a true relationship with Jesus Christ, the author and finisher of our faith.

It doesn't seem like a very even exchange, following a few commands for a lifetime of favor, for healing from sickness and disease and for eternal life. But this is how God works. We give the very little we have and He takes that one tiny seed and allows it to grow into something beautiful. Little is much when God is in it.

Heavenly Father,

Nobody gets out of this life unscathed. And though we may currently be facing a mountain of inexplicable impossibility, we stop right now to give You the highest praise. Thank You for loving us! Thank You for sending Your Son to die for us. Thank You for Your mercy and Your grace! In the good times and the bad, we will humble ourselves before You and simply give THANKS! Hallelujah to the King of kings and Lord of lords! To Him who sits on the right hand of God the Father, we give You praise!

In Jesus's name, amen.

Chapter 6

A HERITAGE OF HEALING

"No weapon formed against you shall prosper, and every tongue which rises against you in judgment you shall condemn. This is the heritage of the servants of the Lord, and their righteousness is from Me," says the Lord.
—Isaiah 54:17

MANY TIMES WE look around and don't think we can possibly survive the storm life has thrust us into. We can't see past the dark clouds surrounding our day. But God.

I have seen healing in my own life and in the lives of many very close to me, as well as miracles that could only have been handed to me compliments of the Almighty.

Growing up in a pastor's home, I have heard about life-threatening situations since I can remember. I have witnessed how frightening situations that make your hair stand on end have turned on a dime when people trusted God with their lives, and how they went terribly awry when they didn't. Though the initial situations can be strikingly similar in nature, our choices (good or bad) can lead us down very different paths.

Satan will try to consume us at our weakest point, and if we have a life-threatening illness, then that is what oftentimes takes precedence in our thought life. It can consume every waking hour if we allow fear to overwhelm us. If we allow fear to leak into even the tiniest crack, we give Satan the opportunity to take our focus off God. At this point it is very easy to lapse into depression or self-pity, sinking into deep despair.

However, if we keep our mind focused on God and trust in Him, Isaiah 26:3 says we will be kept in perfect peace, no matter how out of control our lives may seem. This doesn't mean that every day we live in Utopia, all traffic lights turn green as we drive through town, and our kids follow every direction without hesitation. It means as we face problems that seem to burn the entire infrastructure of our lives to the ground, we can say with confidence, "If God is for us, who can be against us?" (Rom. 8:31). God has promised to gift us with His joy and peace so that we can triumph through any situation without getting an ulcer.

We simply cannot afford to allow the enemy to steal our joy. We can start out the day with a smile on our face, then run into a few snags at lunch, and by dinnertime we have a full-blown war on our hands. The enemy seems to be winning, because we have allowed him to come in and rob us of our peace. By nightfall we start saying things like, "Why me, God? Don't You love me? Why are You doing this to me? Don't You know that I go to church every week?" And just that quickly we have fallen right into Satan's trap, feeling pity instead of praise, looking inward instead of upward. We have lost sight of what is most important in life because we are only focused on the problem.

Psalm 121:1–2 says, "I will lift up my eyes to the hill—from whence comes my help? My help comes from the LORD, who made heaven and earth." When we are in a serious situation, it's time to stop looking around every corner for help. Stop asking for advice from people who haven't had a new idea in the last century. It's time to sit still, be quiet, and look up.

GOD IS IN CONTROL

When I was a teenager, my paternal grandmother was diagnosed with stomach cancer at the age of sixty-nine. Like so many others blindsided by this horrific disease, her tumor was the size of a softball by the time the doctors found it. They predicted the best-case scenario to include a colostomy bag after hours of surgery and a life expectancy not to exceed two years. She would be forced into early retirement from a job she dearly loved, serving lunch at a local school cafeteria. The doctor said she would be in the hospital for weeks and the surgery would last a minimum of four hours.

There was no shortage of bad news in this equation, but the doctor did not know my grandmother. There are two things that defined Vada Hagee: her deep love for the Lord and her matter-of-fact German disposition. You never had to guess (or ask) what she was thinking. And, true to form, as she was being rolled in on the gurney for her life-saving surgery, she let the surgeon know that he was not the one in control; God was. I'm sure this did a lot for the doctor's self-esteem, but the fact of the matter was that Grandma just didn't care. She wanted the doctor to be on alert that angels were surrounding her and everything was going to be just fine, no matter what the medical facts might be.

Her family members and friends gathered at the hospital and started praying. Vada Hagee had been the epitome of an active preacher's wife. Truth be told, she could preach (or teach) circles around my grandfather any day of the week.

As children we would gather in her kitchen, placing our chairs in a circular formation in front of her pantry door that was covered in a fine, green felt fabric. One by one Grandma would pull out the much-loved paper Bible characters she had made to tell us every Bible story until we could recount them ourselves...using the same paper people. For her there was no substitution for learning the Word of God, and there were no excuses for not honoring it. There were no areas of gray for Grandma Hagee; the lines were clearly drawn.

And this is just how she went into her surgery. The battle lines were clearly drawn. There was no room for defeat or doubt to linger. She had already claimed the victory on the way in to surgery, not having any definitive idea of the outcome. She just believed from her very core that if God was on her side, no bad news from the doctor could get in her way. This was just a tiny speed bump on her way to something bigger and better.

At the onset of the surgery everyone had great faith that she would recover, but no one could say for sure the toll cancer would take on her life. The daunting words of the surgeon didn't leave much hope for a bright or overly fulfilling future.

An hour and a half later (not four hours as predicted) the surgeon walked through the doors separating the surgical wing from the waiting room. As the words spilled out, we knew that God had once again shown up in a very real way, leaving us nothing but thankful. There was no denying the miracle that had just taken place. No complications. No permanent colostomy bag. The cancer was contained, and no follow-up surgeries or further cancer treatments were necessary. The two-year limit previously placed on my grandmother's life was extended to a limitless life full of honoring her Redeemer. God had stepped in and once again shown off with His amazing grace for His faithful servant Vada Hagee.

Grandma knew that God was not finished with her yet. God's perfect peace surrounded her like a comforting cloud from the time she was diagnosed until the surgeon came out in blue scrubs to deliver the two words every oncology patient waits with bated breath to hear—cancer free (Isa. 26:3). Two weeks later she went right back to work.

YOUR LATTER WILL BE GREATER

In his late sixties my dad went to the doctor's office for a routine checkup and came out needing a quadruple bypass. (Go big or go home, right?)

Once again, when we found out there was going to be another surgery in our family, we circled the wagons and started immediately covering Dad in prayer. Just like his mother, going into the procedure he had every confidence that the surgery would be nothing short of a complete success. Before the first surgical cut was made, we had already started giving thanks to God for the complete healing that was on the way. There simply was no room for fear or doubt or for Satan to elbow his way into the equation.

Of course, with every surgery comes the never-ending waiting period. Dad was ushered into the surgical suite, and we started reading Psalm 91, one of my grandmother's favorite scriptures. Verse 11 says, "For He shall give His angels charge over you, to keep you in all your ways." As a family we knew that even though we weren't allowed to physically enter the room where the surgery was taking place (and believe me, if there was a way, Diana Hagee would have found it), the angels had already gone ahead to pave the way.

We were camped out in two conference rooms at the hospital with various family members and close friends. My father's dear friend, Rabbi Scheinberg, was there along with other pastors from around the country. In one room, Rabbi was reading Scripture and passing the Bible around to others who wanted to join in. As they read through the Psalms, interceding on my father's behalf, you could literally feel the presence of the Holy Spirit saturate the room.

When God is in the room, there is no denying His presence. There was a calm peace about the room and a feeling of absolute comfort, the comfort found only in knowing that God is in control.

The Bible continued to be passed around the table as each reader began to speak blessings of healing over my dad. We set that prayer room on fire! The presence of God coated every corner of the room.

In the next room we set up a hospitality station where we could wait, talk, and eat. It was a very strange day for me, as I had in recent years been the one on the operating table or in the treatment room while the others waited for my results. I almost didn't know what to do with myself.

My dad has always been the "rock" for our family, and now he was the one needing our support.

In my mind I could see my dad giving the doctors a big thumbs-up at the end of the surgery, barely awake after the anesthesia. I wouldn't be shocked if he went into the surgery suite and gave the doctors final instructions or asked the nurse to order some fried chicken for his dinner. I just knew he would feel *that* great by the end of the day.

And yet, while God was busy restoring his health, we were busy waiting.

Every minute seemed to last an hour, every hour an eternity, but eventually good reports started coming in from the surgeon. Was I surprised that the surgery was coming along perfectly? No. Everything my dad puts his hand to, he does with exhaustive excellence. Why should open-heart surgery be any different?

There were more prayer and more sandwiches as the minutes clicked by at a painfully slow pace. Finally the wait was over, and the surgeon announced the good news we all had been anxiously awaiting. Though we had no doubt God was orchestrating this event from start to finish, it is always refreshing to hear that final confirmation. It's almost like hearing God say, "Umm, I told you so." And just like that, you release the breath you didn't even know you were holding.

God showed up once again, and our first reaction was to collectively give thanks (1 Chron. 16:34). "Thank You for revealing this unknown health issue. Thank You for guiding the surgeon's hand. Thank You for friends who are willing to lift us up in prayer. And thank You for complete healing." We rejoiced in the goodness of the Lord (Phil. 4:4). What Satan had meant for evil, God had used for His glory.

The end result was a quadruple bypass, but there were no complications. Dad was out of the office for five short weeks, then he went right back to working around the clock. He was restored so that his latter days have been greater than his former (Job 42:12). He now feels better than he has in years, with more energy than ever to do what he loves most—spreading the gospel to all the world (Matt. 28:19). For someone whose lifestyle is full speed ahead in his sleep, this was a miracle all its own.

We all breathed a collective sigh of relief when this was behind us as a family. Surely it was time to celebrate and relax, let our hair down and just enjoy this perfect moment of complete triumph. I mean, what else could possibly go wrong?

Just when we thought it was safe to swim at the beach (*Jaws* theme music here), out pops that nasty gray fin. Six weeks after my dad's bypass Diana was diagnosed with invasive carcinoma cells in her breast tissue. This was one of those years where you just had to roll with the punches and admit that life had become like Baskin-Robbins ice cream...thirty-one flavors of crazy. I am grateful that, like my dad, Diana has had a miraculous recovery from a double mastectomy and is leading a limitless, cancer-free life, serving the Lord in her position as pastor's wife of Cornerstone Church, special events director, and so much more.

LET GOD INVADE YOUR LIFE

I hope you can see from these examples that it doesn't matter your age or the stage of life you are entering (Acts 10:34–35). God sees you and understands your needs on a far greater scale than you could ever imagine in your wildest dreams. No matter who or where you are, He is stretching His arm out to you, offering that which your heart desires. He wants to give you the thing you need most, even if you don't even know exactly what it is. He has your very best interests in mind, and He can move heaven and earth to restore what you have lost. Taste and see that the Lord is good.

If you will allow God the opportunity to invade your life, you will be amazed at the divine destiny He has carved out just for you. Draw close to Him, and He will draw close to you (James 4:8).

Heavenly Father,

Satan is a liar, and he comes to rob, to kill, and to destroy. Father God, we ask that You would surround us with life. We choose blessings and not curses, life and not death. We ask that when the devourer makes threats against our lives, when he plants fear in our minds or tells us that we aren't good enough to be loved by someone as wonderful as You, that we don't deserve Your healing touch—go before us and be our rear guard. May Your outstretched arm grant us unlimited favor as a child of God. We know that every demon trembles at the mention of the name of Jehovah Rophe, the Lord who heals. We do not take good health for granted. For we are fearfully and wonderfully made in Your image, created to be more than conquerors through Jesus Christ. May our lives glorify You in all that we say and do.

In Jesus's name, amen.

Chapter 7

DIVINE INTERVENTION

*Because he has set his love upon Me, therefore I
will deliver him; I will set him on high, because he
has known My name. He shall call upon Me, and
I will answer him; I will be with him in trouble;
I will deliver him and honor him. With long life
I will satisfy him, and show him My salvation.*

—PSALM 91:14–16

HOW DO WE invite God to intervene on our behalf?
Is it truly just as simple as asking?

I think the Bible may have been the first book
in the Dummies series: *Life's Road Map for Dummies.* I love
that God illustrates important lessons over and over again,
just in case we didn't understand the first twenty times. He
retells a story from so many different angles that there is
no way to miss the meaning.

Several times throughout Scripture God gives us specific
instruction to call upon Him. We are to call out in the day
of trouble, seeking Him with our whole heart. Anyone who
has invited Jesus Christ into his or her life and accepted
Him as his or her Savior is welcome to call upon His name
at any time. When we hand our shattered lives over to the

Lord, He has promised to satisfy us with long life here on earth as well as eternal life with Him—quite an amazing gift on the other side of asking for a favor.

He is as close as the mention of His name. When you have a big need, you want to call on someone who can act quickly and with authority. You want someone who can hold your hand through the darkest day and in whom you can place your complete trust...especially when your life depends upon it.

Don't Blink

When my siblings and I were very young, my family loved loading up the car and spending Saturday afternoon at the movies. (Think of the funky paneled station wagon from any Chevy Chase movie, stuffed full of kids, and you have pretty much nailed it.) I don't know what would possess someone to take five kids to the movies, but we did it almost every week...many weeks we even took friends. We probably could have qualified for a group rate all on our own.

As a child I thought going to the movies was just about the coolest thing you could do. Our normal Saturday movie routine included Dad taking my two younger brothers into the theater to save seats. Diana would take the three girls (myself included) to buy popcorn and soda, and eventually we would meet up with the boys at our seats.

On one particular Saturday we piled out of the station wagon and headed straight to the theater lobby to play video games (which usually meant putting pennies in the machine and watching the test pattern because we didn't know any better). After we played a few rounds of Ms.

Pac-Man, my dad would whistle and all five of us would immediately stop what we were doing and either head for the theater or concession stand. It was the well-known whistle no one dared to disobey.

Somewhere between the games, snacks, and theater my youngest sister, Sandy, disappeared. As a child, all I knew was that one second we were waiting for candy bars and the next second my parents were in meltdown mode. I had no idea how horrifying the situation was at the time; I only knew that no one could locate my sister.

Diana ran into the theater to let Dad know Sandy was missing. True to form, he immediately flew into action and ran to the lobby. He screamed, "Lock the doors!" At that moment I knew we were in *big* trouble. The tone of his voice told me this was serious business. If you understood the dialect of Dad, it also meant, "Don't mess with me."

As the manager ran up and tried to calm him, it only fueled the fire. I almost felt sorry for the manager, who clearly had no idea what he was up against. "Lock the doors *right now*." Dad began to yell out the description of my sister, letting everyone around know that she was missing. No one would be leaving until my sister was found.

"Short, dark brown hair. Brown eyes. Just under three feet tall. Wearing shorts and a yellow T-shirt."

Other than my dad yelling, you could have heard a pin drop. I was standing with only three of the five siblings in a very surreal moment where people were helplessly staring at us, popcorn in hand. Surely this wasn't happening.

And yet it was. By now Diana was running in and out of the theaters calling Sandy's name in the off chance she was lost. No one believed that she had wandered away, because everyone had heard Dad's whistle. Sandy would have *never* ignored "the whistle."

By now we were all looking for Sandy while Dad made sure that the entire theater remained on lock-down status. The manager had quickly ascertained that he was no longer in control. We continued looking in every bathroom stall, opening every door twice, checking inside of every cabinet and wandering through every passageway we could find. Nothing was off limits. Where in the world could she be? Was she gone forever? It was really too much to absorb.

Having looked everywhere four children could, my three siblings and I stood helplessly by, watching our parents play out a torturous scene that seemed to take days. Dad told Diana to check the bathrooms one more time. In one last, desperate attempt to find her baby daughter, she started retracing every step.

She went in and out of every stall, hoping against hope, continuing to pray that God would make a way. As she looked in the last handicap stall, there was Sandy standing on top of the toilet seat. Her wide-open eyes told the story.

"Mommy, the lady said she wouldn't hurt me if I didn't scream."

Diana held her and cried, giving thanks to the Lord for His merciful protection with every breath. And just like that, our family was made whole once again through the unmerited mercy of a loving God.

I have not often dared to relive that day or even to think about all of the things that might have happened if the circumstances were different. The pain is too deep to think about a life without my sister. The older I get, the more thankful I am for God's provision, for His faithfulness, for His love, and for His mercy that is new each and every day.

As a child I didn't think of the endless possibilities that could have taken place that day. I simply wanted to know where my sister had gone and when I would be seeing her again. As a parent my perspective is entirely different. I cannot even allow myself to think about it.

If God had not supernaturally intervened that day, the consequences could have been catastrophic. My parents cried out to God in a day that, by any other measure, could have been the end of our family as we knew it. But God leaned down and said, "I hear you! I got this one! I see that My children need Me, and I am going to intervene on their behalf. I'm not sending My angels to do this job; I'm going to take care of this one Myself." There was no denying that without God's divine intervention, our day could have ended on a very sour note.

Life is like that. Things can change drastically in the blink of an eye. Problems can smack you right in the face when you least expect them. What will you do when they come? Where will you turn when no human force can give you the results that will make the difference between life and death, between the loss of a loved one or spending several more years with them?

Divine intervention can take place anywhere and at any time. God may not respond in your thirty-second time limit, but if you continue to seek His face, He is faithful to respond with the perfect outcome for your particular brand of nightmare.

A DIVINE REVERSAL

I would like to introduce my sweet friend Vicki, who trusted God to intervene when her health started failing. I have known Vicki most of my life, and we have literally grown up in church together. There has never been a time when she wasn't active in every possible church function. I don't mean she is the person bringing the napkins to the church picnic; I mean she is the one hosting the weekly Bible study, singing at the woman's event, organizing the Women of Wisdom group for her church. She ministers to the children's Sunday school classes through the use of colorful puppets and cohosts an annual event to feed and clothe those less fortunate, all the while telling them the salvation message.

I could fill the next chapter with things Vicki has done to go out of her way to reach out to others (never expecting anything in return), but hopefully you get the idea. She is not a wallflower who sits idly by waiting for someone else to do the nitty-gritty work. She jumps right in, rolls up her sleeves, and makes things happen.

Vicki's story is another example of challenging things happening to God's people while still living under the mantle of favor. If you are of the camp that thinks Christians who are true believers never have bad things happen to them, then hopefully this example will successfully illustrate how God's amazing grace can carry you through a tough time when you hand your problems over to the Master. Yes, God's people have problems too. Shocker!

At the beginning of 2008 Vicki felt like her body was in such a state of deterioration that she would not live through the next few years to see her daughter graduate from high school. She was more than one hundred pounds overweight and was what medical science would consider morbidly obese. (I would never say this myself, because I love Vicki no matter what size or shape, but I use this term so that you can understand the true sense of the obstacle my friend was trying to overcome. This was a Texas-size problem.)

Vicki began to earnestly seek God on which medical route would work best to save her life. Which way should she turn? Leaving her beloved daughter and husband behind was not an option!

Vicki contacted a bariatric surgeon and discussed the possibility of having gastric bypass surgery. Insurance refused to cover the surgery, so Vicki and her husband began to pray that God would make a way where there seemed to be no way if this was His will for Vicki. When you are in the middle of a crisis, He is the way maker. In John 14:6 Jesus says, "I am the way, the truth, and the life." Vicki knew that He would make a way and give her a new, fulfilling, and healthy life so that she could enjoy many more years with the family she so dearly loved.

After much prayer and fasting, it was evident that this bypass surgery was not the road for her to take, so they thanked God for that answer (without questioning why) and continued praying that God would reveal His perfect plan for Vicki's life. God's delays are not God's denials. And while the bypass surgery wasn't the answer, it didn't mean that God was out of ideas.

The couple continued to pray together, and in late April Vicki's husband, Ike, woke up in the middle of the night and felt the Holy Spirit clearly direct him to contact Dr.

Welch, an endocrinologist. (Just a side note: Ike is my pediatrician, one of the world's most patient and loving individuals. Words are not enough to express how phenomenal he is with my girls. If my husband would allow it, I would erect a statue of Dr. Pauli in our yard. That's just how much we love him.) Ike's practice is located in the same building as Dr. Welch's. However, since Ike is a pediatrician and Dr. Welch is an adult endocrinologist, there would be no professional reason for him to contact her. God simply placed her name on his heart and gave them the direction they were seeking for Vicki.

Even though her practice was full, Dr. Welch agreed to take Vicki on as a new patient, and they met the following month for the very first time. Vicki was welcomed with open arms and a myriad of diagnostic tests. What could be better? Sadly, the results confirmed what Vicki already knew. If they could not get her various physical issues under control, she would not live more than five years. The thundercloud that was hiding under the surface started pouring rain once again.

On May 8, 2008, Vicki received her official diagnosis—dysmetabolic syndrome, a potentially fatal disease. This syndrome includes a little bit of everything: hypertension, high blood sugar, high triglycerides, low good cholesterol, and high risk for heart attack or stroke. There was no positive spin on this diagnosis.

Vicki and Ike continued to fast and pray, asking for wisdom and direction. Having worked in and around church ministry all of their lives, they had seen firsthand the awesome power of Jesus Christ. There was no doubt in their minds that what God had done for others He could certainly do for Vicki. But would the answer come soon enough to save her?

Vicki knew the road ahead would be an uphill battle, but she believed in the absolute power of the Almighty and armed herself with continuous prayer, meditating on the Word day and night (Ps. 1:2). She also contacted a few close friends and family members to act as prayer warriors and stand in the gap for her, lifting her before the throne and believing that in Christ all things are possible (Gal. 6:2).

When her journey began, Vicki weighed 255 pounds, her triglycerides were dangerously high at 600, her cholesterol was at 230, her high-density lipids (the good cholesterol) were at 8, and her low-density lipids (the bad cholesterol) were at 169. You don't have to be a medical student to understand the seriousness of this situation.

Vicki made a daily regimen of praying and following every order the doctor gave her to the finest detail. She knew that God would do His part, but she wanted to put her very best foot forward. She was not going down without a fight! She hired a personal trainer and began a weekly workout routine that pushed her body to new physical limits but increased her stamina.

Over the next three and a half years her diligence paid off. She lost eighty pounds and started to see great improvement in her blood work. During this time Vicki and Ike went to the executive pastor of our church, (my brother) Pastor Matthew Hagee, and asked him for prayer.

During a Bible study at the church conducted by my brother, Matthew marched right down the aisle, looked Vicki in the face, and said, "You asked us to pray for you; well, here I am." Then he anointed her head with oil (James

5:14–15). Hope sprung up inside of Vicki like a gushing spring on a dry summer day. The peace that surpasses all understanding began to saturate her very being, and she knew that God had her under His sheltering wing.

Isn't it awesome when God reveals Himself to us? When He just gives us that frozen moment in time to know that we are ultimately the most important thing on His agenda?

Vicki continued to throw herself into a total health makeover, but she received more crushing news from the doctor's office. No matter how hard she tried, this was as good as it would get for her; there would be no return to her former quality of life. She would need medication for the rest of her life just to survive, so she might as well get used to living with dysmetabolic syndrome. Even though her triglycerides were at 197 and every number on her statistic sheet was improving with each passing month, the news was less than stellar.

Vicki wasn't about to accept this for one second! She had received the anointing and believed that God had something better for her. The Bible says, "Let the redeemed of the LORD say so" (Ps. 107:2). Vicki was redeemed by the blood of Jesus Christ at the cross and was not about to let a doctor's report label her as a victim for life. John 10:10 says, "I have come that they might have life, and that they might have it more abundantly." Vicki was accepting nothing less than *total* abundance. Christ had conquered sickness and disease at the cross, and Vicki was clinging to the promises God had given to her personally in His Word.

Vicki knew the only way she would completely conquer this physical demon was to ask God for divine intervention. Vicki and her husband would not accept what medical science was telling them! They cried out to the name that is above every other name (Phil. 2:9–11), the name that causes demons to tremble and diseases to flee. It would be this name that would carry her down a road to complete healing.

In October of 2011 Vicki celebrated her fiftieth birthday, a huge milestone after her original diagnosis. As she continued to celebrate the goodness of the Lord, her phone rang. A dear friend wanted to read Leviticus 23, telling Vicki that this would be *her* year of personal jubilee; all that had been lost would be restored (Joel 2:25). Together they claimed this victory over her health, and Vicki knew this was another piece to the long-awaited answer she so desperately needed. She was anxious to see God's plan unfold.

As soon as this victory was proclaimed, the enemy showed up in spades trying to discourage her. The following month she began to gain weight again. Every doctor she had consulted (endocrinologist, gynecologist, internist) agreed that a large amount of abdominal fat could not be lost through further diet and exercise; it would need to be removed surgically. Again, Vicki and Ike were on their faces asking God for divine intervention, asking for financial provision for a necessary surgery that was (once again) not covered by insurance. God provided, and the surgery was scheduled for November 29, 2011.

Over eleven pounds of fat was removed. For the next two painful months Vicki recovered at home, unable to exercise or take the medications previously prescribed. She continued her daily regimen of prayer and meditation until her follow-up appointment in February, never doubting that her answer was on the way. Still, she was understandably apprehensive to hear the results as she had been ordered to temporarily stop taking her medication until after her surgery. What would her blood work look like? Would her lack of medication cause her a significant medical setback?

The week before Vicki was to receive her updated test results, her pastor (my dad), John Hagee, preached on receiving God's blessing after giving the firstfruits offering (Prov. 3:9). What is a "firstfruits" offering? Proverbs gives a full explanation, but basically this means that you seek God first in all you do. When you give to Him, you offer Him the first and best of everything. You offer Him the first portion of your paycheck before paying off everybody else. It is putting Matthew 6:33 into action and seeking first the kingdom of God. When you put God first, He promises to reward you with showers of blessings.

Vicki's husband, Ike, is a dedicated pediatrician during the week and volunteers his weekends to the church when he isn't on call at the office. Every Sunday morning Ike films the service in the main sanctuary for the television audience. This Sunday Dad was speaking on firstfruits. So Ike was filming that day as my dad spoke about different ways God wants to bless our lives, if we will only allow Him the privilege of doing so. And actually, the privilege is all ours.

As it turned out, Vicki and Ike had been praying for several personal breakthroughs in their lives, many of which centered around financial issues; so, feeling led by the Holy Spirit, they decided to participate in this firstfruits offering, above and beyond their normal tithe.

Let me be very clear here. They were both seeking God's will for their lives *first*, above all else. They wanted Him to saturate their lives like never before and to send them in the perfect direction that would bring Him honor. They were not donating extra money to pay God off, as if He requires a deductible for His health plan or a down payment on a blessing.

If God had asked them to donate five hours of their time to feed the homeless, I'm sure they would have done it without question. But God laid on both of their hearts to give a certain amount of money, and they were faithful to do what they felt God was requesting. I want to make sure you understand I'm not talking about a quick fix, name-it-and-claim-it prosperity doctrine. I'm simply talking about what Samuel did in the Bible (1 Sam. 3:7–11). "Speak, Lord, for Your servant is listening."

They went home and continued praying for financial breakthroughs, not even concentrating on Vicki's health issues at this point. They were looking for God to saturate every facet of their lives and began playing healing Scriptures night and day throughout their home. They wanted God to know that *whatever* He had in store for them, they were ready to receive it.

And don't you know, it's just like God to show up when we least expect Him? To show up and show off! Just a few days later Vicki went in for another routine checkup. But this would be no routine report. It was the day for God to bless Vicki exceedingly, abundantly above all that she could ask, think, or imagine (Eph. 3:20–21). It was the day that her blood work came back totally clean, and Vicki knew that her prayers were answered. The numbers on her medical chart had notably shrunk: triglycerides were 68, cholesterol was 197, high-density lipids were 73.4, and low-density lipids were 109.

I give the exact numbers for those of you who like to see proof. And I annotate dates throughout the timeline so that you can understand we serve an on-time God. Sometimes we have to persevere, waiting years for God's perfect answer. Sometimes (not as often as I would like) we receive an answer immediately, but there is *never* a time when God does not answer us when we diligently seek Him (Prov. 8:17). We may not be in love with the answer He gives us, but He is faithful to respond to our petitions.

We are in such a hurry with our lives that we want to press A1 and ask God to immediately drop potato chips from His great vending machine in the sky...along with a large miracle. But God is telling us that He needs more of our time than just a quick snack break. What happens when we have a problem? We seek God night and day, fast a few meals maybe, and even crack open our Bibles. But what happens when the problem is resolved? Do we continue to seek Him with that much intensity, or do we decide that church attendance on Sundays is enough? God knows where to find us if He needs us.

There are others who believe if we do anything to "help God out," then we must not be spiritual or godly enough. The Bible says that if we seek Him first, He is faithful to help us navigate the difficult stretches that take us down life's winding pathway (Matt. 6:33). We don't have to face the giant alone, but we should definitely be an active part of our solution.

John 14:21 says, "He who has My commandments and keeps them, it is he who loves Me. And he who loves Me will be loved by My Father, and I will love him and manifest Myself to him."

When we follow God's commands, we are showing God that we love Him and respect His Word. We are actively inviting Him to participate in our lives.

If Vicki would have sat on her couch and eaten doughnuts all day long, then five years from now she couldn't cry out to God and say, "What happened?" She would need to look no further than her mirror for that answer. But Vicki did as God commanded her, never giving up on the journey as it unfolded around her, and was rewarded with a second chance at an unlimited life.

Vicki's ending is one of biblical proportion, no less than the woman with the issue of blood. During Vicki's last appointment the doctor was so pleased with her blood work that she actually did a happy dance right there in the office. And with this dance she delivered the news Vicki had been waiting years to hear...the dysmetabolic syndrome had been totally reversed.

> Oh, give thanks to the LORD, for He is good!
> For His mercy endures forever.
> —PSALM 118:29

Heavenly Father,

Thank You, God, that You are with us in our day of trouble. Thank You for being as close as the mention of Your name and for Your faithfulness to stop the enemy in his tracks. How great is the sum of your thoughts toward us, O Lord, that You would surround us with angels to guard us and keep us safe. What Satan means for evil You can use for good. Thank You for hearing us when we call. When our spirits are overwhelmed, You are only a whisper away. May Your outstretched arm protect us in our day of trouble, as we give You all praise, honor, and glory for the good things You have done in our lives. We praise You for the victories You have given us and for those that are already on the way!

In Jesus's name, amen.

Chapter 8

MERCY-FULL

If I say, "My foot slips," Your mercy, O Lord,
will hold me up. In the multitude of my anxi-
eties within me, Your comforts delight my soul.
—PSALM 94:18–19

HAVE YOU EVER had a problem that you felt might completely consume you? Just swallow you whole as the great fish did with Jonah? I have great news! God's mercy endures to *all* generations. Numbers 14:18 says that His mercy is abundant, and 1 Chronicles 16:34 says that it endures forever. Psalm 100:5 says His mercy is everlasting.

Mercy is literally peppered throughout the entire Bible, but let's talk a little about the mercy we *all* gained at the Cross. Everything in Scripture is either sacrificed or redeemed. Animals were sacrificed for human sins, and Jesus was sacrificed to take away the sins of the world, to completely redeem us so that we wouldn't have to die for our own sins.

There was Jesus, being nailed to a cross by Roman centurions who despised Him for no discernible reason. An enraged crowd demanded that a murderer go free, and

Jesus was handed over to them. People were chanting, "Crucify Him! Crucify Him!" And Pilate handed Jesus over, even after proclaiming Him to be blameless and without fault of any kind. Pilate washed his hands, and thus Jesus's fate was sealed in Rome's court. There was no appeal.

As the manic crowd took control and started marching toward Calvary, Luke records that the soldiers began to taunt Jesus. "If You are the Christ, save Yourself." It was the worst kind of flash mob.

And still Jesus kept walking underneath the heavy weight of the cross, the seemingly unbearable weight of the sins of the world. Think about that for a minute: carrying the sins of the entire universe on your shoulders and knowing this is your divine destiny; blood running down your face, dust covering your sandals that are slipping on the cobblestone streets, and your back breaking from the dead weight of a wooden cross.

Right here you would have lost me. I would have been up in a cloud of smoke, telling these idiots they could pay for their own sins and suffer the consequences of their own foolish choices. At the very least I would be making a list of those who were actively participating in my demise and calling me names. No, sir, they would not be seeing the inside of *my* pearly gates.

But God in His infinite mercy allowed His *only* Son to die for us...even as we mocked and ridiculed Him in the final hours of His life on earth. This scene was a grand parade of buffoons on display, refusing to admit that Jesus came to earth of His own free will and volition, born to be our Savior and redeem all mankind, and born to die in our place. It would have been so much easier to allow us to destroy ourselves, but mercy was granted in abundance.

At the end of the Via Dolorosa (the long and winding road Jesus traveled through the city) was Golgotha. Jesus's reward for making it this far was to be nailed to the very same cross He had carried, hung between two thieves. Jesus was without sin, and yet He was placed between two men who were receiving their just punishment for crimes they had actually committed.

He could have called a host of angels to take Him off the cross and thumbed His nose at the entire crowd, but He chose our redemption over His comfort, over His reputation, over His own personal needs and desires, over His earthly family who sat at the bottom of the cross and watched the dearest on earth be brutally slain...

One thief was quick to jump on the bandwagon, blaspheming Jesus until his very last breath. (What a bummer when he took the next one, huh?) The second thief ridiculed the first, saying that they were receiving their just punishment, but Jesus was blameless. He recognized Jesus as His Savior.

Then what did Jesus say to the thief? "Assuredly, I say to you, today you will be with Me in Paradise" (Luke 23:43). And when Jesus went to be with His Father in heaven, this thief joined Him, forever washed white as snow, with sins that were never remembered again. That, my friend, is the true picture of mercy.

Trying to measure God's mercy is like measuring drops of water in the ocean or grains of sand in the desert. It is like the cupcakes, candy bars, and endless desserts that suddenly appear on every flat surface when you are on a diet and trying to avoid sugar. You can't ignore God's mercy. When He gives it to you, there is no doubt the source from which it came. It is a sweet fragrance that coats your life, and you can't help but feel pure, unadulterated peace. If God can forgive the thief on the cross for a lifetime of sin, He can surely forgive you.

THE BRILLIANCE AND BEAUTY OF THE CROSS

I constantly hear disgruntled people saying, "I can't believe he did that to me." Or, "I can't believe she's like that." Why not? These are flawed people we are talking about. All of us have flaws. This is the brilliance and beauty of the cross. All of our collective flaws were completely redeemed so that when we have a crisis we can turn to the One who said, "It is finished!"

What was finished? The sting of death. Sickness and disease. All riches in heaven and earth belong to the Lord. Satan no longer had any authority.

Yes, people are ridiculously disappointing on a consistent basis, but so what? When your peeps remind you of what you don't deserve, remind them that you are redeemed by Christ's blood that flowed from the cross. That is mercy. With those two pieces of wood, each one of us became an instant victor. We no longer have to pander to those who only wish negativity upon our lives. We have the freedom to walk away. We are covered by God's grace, wrapped in His peace, and drowning in His unlimited mercy.

Having survived cancer, kids, and coworkers, I know that God can dole out mercy like no one else. There's no doubt in my mind (Ps. 31:14). When you have a big problem, you will find no greater source of help.

Unlike other varieties of help, this brand doesn't come with a reminder of what you didn't achieve in high school, how you acted out when you were twelve, or that you chose the wrong career path. It is simply a gift. "For everyone who asks receives" (Matt. 7:8).

However, if you don't ask God for something, He can't give it to you. Think of it like this. If you don't breathe in fresh air, your lungs cannot get oxygen to the rest of your body, no matter how desperate the need is. You have to ask for God's help. Then breathe in His goodness, trusting that His plan is better than the one you dreamed up late last night after eating too many chili dogs.

Psalm 103:17–18 says, "But the mercy of the LORD is from everlasting to everlasting upon them that fear him, and his righteousness unto children's children; to such as keep his covenant, and to those that remember his commandments to do them" (KJV).

God wants your life to be dripping with mercy, literally coated from the inside out. But He cannot dispense one drop until you make Him the Lord of your life, until you keep His covenants and follow His commandments. Once you figure out this simple recipe for success, your life will become richer than ever before.

IF THE LOAD IS TOO HEAVY, ASK FOR HELP

One day my (then) eight-year-old daughter, Kassi, came into the kitchen while I was cooking. She loves to help cook anything and often comes up with her own concoctions that are (upon occasion) edible. One of the things I love most about Kassi is that she is completely unafraid to try new things. She doesn't limit herself because of the opinions of those around her. She just lives life with gusto and accomplishes most of what she puts her mind to because she's not afraid of failure.

On this occasion I asked her to take out the trash before we got started in the kitchen. "Kassi, if the bag is too heavy, just let me know and I will carry it for you." Being independent by nature, she assured me that she could do it herself.

A few seconds later she came back into the kitchen with an apologetic expression on her face, and I could almost dictate the words before they tumbled out of her mouth.

"Mom, I'm so sorry I spilled the trash everywhere. It was just too heavy for me."

"Kassi, it was an accident. Don't worry about it. We will go outside and clean it up together."

As I walked out my front door, broom in hand, I saw trash strewn from my front doorstep, down the porch, and around the side of my house to the trash can. Kassi was trying so hard to do the right thing, but the load was just too heavy.

Sometimes in life we are handed a load that is too heavy to carry on our own. In a flash we are given devastating news that could irrevocably change our lives. Being human, we grab that big sack of trash and try to drag it along the journey to where we think it belongs, where we think we will find relief. Along the way we are spilling our garbage everywhere, and by the time we get to where we are going, we are out of gas and the problem we were trying to rid ourselves of has spewed itself all over every area of our lives. It has consumed us and polluted our journey.

All Kassi had to do was ask for my help. All we have to do is ask God to help carry our load. "God, please take this giant problem from me because the load is too heavy and I can't do it without You." That's it. His mercy will hold us up. We walk along life's journey and God carries our trash. He decides where to dump it, and we simply trust Him with the disposal so that we don't continue to "own" all of the garbage in our lives.

Sometimes when life seems overwhelming, or maybe a little too much of a good thing, I sit and sort it out. It's like eating the elephant one bite at a time. Maybe you can't tackle the entire thing at once, but in smaller chunks anything is digestible.

SORT IT OUT

"SORT it out." The S stands for "Be *still*." Psalm 46:10–11 says, "Be still, and know that I am God; I will be exalted among the nations, I will be exalted in the earth! The LORD of hosts is with us; the God of Jacob is our refuge."

My dad tells the story of a young girl who was playing outside in her front yard with a large group of children. Her ball had rolled into the street, and throwing caution to the wind, she began to run full-speed toward the street at the same time a car came barreling around the corner. Her father saw the impending threat and immediately yelled at her to stop.

Normally this stubborn girl would have continued running, but for some reason this time she stopped immediately and without question. Listening to that one word,

"STOP!", saved her life. Sometimes we just need to be still and listen to our Father's voice. We may not see the potentially fatal danger up ahead, but if we listen and heed the warning, it could spare us a great deal of pain.

When life hands you a steaming plate of crazy, sometimes it helps to sit down and take a deep breath. Nothing is as big as it initially seems, and a problem shared with the Creator isn't really anything more than a chance to grow. Sometimes you need to listen to the Father's voice and stop doing what you want for a moment. It might save your life.

The O stands for "Be *optimistic*." Psalm 16:9, 11 says, "Therefore my heart is glad, and my glory rejoices; my flesh also will rest in hope.... You will show me the path of life; in Your presence is fullness of joy; at Your right hand are pleasures forevermore."

If you believe that you deserve God's very best, you will be more likely to seek it out and less likely to limit your own success. With a positive attitude your options are limitless.

Believe you deserve to walk in divine favor. "You have granted me life and favor, and Your care has preserved my spirit" (Job 10:12). Once you understand the depth of God's love, you will never doubt for a second how very deeply He desires your personal success. Don't give away this precious gift just because some other person convinced you that you're not worthy. Stand up and proclaim that you are a child of God and accept that you are a royal heir to the throne, redeemed by the blood of Jesus Christ.

The R stands for "Be *resilient*." Grow deep roots in a solid foundation, and when the storms come you will not be swayed. You can bend, but not break. You can be like a Teflon frying pan, letting everything just slide off when you are caught in one of life's heated moments.

My youngest daughter, Kassidee, is a great example of resilience. No matter what lands on her plate, she rolls with the punches. Children develop amazing character traits very early in life; it is up to us to encourage them to succeed in the areas in which they excel (Prov. 22:6). Concentrate on the good in their lives, and downplay the bad. The world is full of people who will attack them, firing off scathing words from which they might never recover without your sheltering arm. Be their biggest cheerleader, acting as if they could take on the world with their own winning smile. Encourage them to be the unique gift God has created them to be.

The T stands for "Be *thankful*." In my household we are immeasurably thankful for our many blessings, doing our level best to never take anything or anyone for granted. God has so richly bestowed His love and mercy upon us. How can you ever say thank you enough for something of this magnitude?

The second a problem falls into our laps, we begin to praise God for the answer that is sure to come. Our lives have taken us up steep mountains and down painful valleys, but always right where we needed to be.

"Thank you" is such a weak phrase when talking to the One who holds your very next breath and who counts the hairs on your head. The next time you are having a bad day, start looking at the insurmountable evidence of His greatness that saturates your life and realize that the Son is always shining. "Give thanks to the LORD, for He is good! For His mercy endures forever" (Ps. 136:1)!

Heavenly Father,

You are the Chief Cornerstone, precious and elect in Zion. Thank You that when our lives are a complete disaster, we can lean on You. For in our weakness You are strong. You always have our very best in mind, even when we can't begin to understand what that might be or the purpose behind a trial we are facing. We ask that You use us for Your glory, that we might be granted an eternity to praise You. We lift our eyes to the hills, from whence cometh our Redeemer. We lay our concerns at Your feet, knowing the load is too heavy to carry alone. We ask that You handle those things that concern us most, for there is no shadow of turning in You. You are El Shaddai, Almighty God. We put our trust in You.

In Jesus's name, amen.

Chapter 9

GOD SEES

Then she called the name of the Lord who
spoke to her, You-Are-the-God-Who-Sees...
—GENESIS 16:13

THE JEWISH WORD for "God sees" is *El Roi*. This literally means a God who sees everything and is therefore never taken by surprise.

Have you ever had a day that took you by surprise? Sometimes these are welcome surprises, things we are thrilled and blessed to have in our lives: job promotions, a baby on the way, finding a long-lost friend, the long-awaited answer to a problem... But the surprises I would like to discuss here are the gut-wrenching shocks that leave us reeling and gasping for air, hanging by the proverbial thread. It's the punch to the gut that we didn't see coming.

Isn't it reassuring to know that when we are left wondering which way is up, there is a source of help that was not shocked at all by our circumstances? Revelation 22:13 tells us that He is the Alpha and the Omega, the beginning and the end. This means that there has never been a time when God did not exist, and there is no end to His existence.

Psalm 37:23–24 says, "The steps of a good man are ordered by the LORD, and He delights in his way. Though he fall, he shall not be utterly cast down; for the LORD upholds him with His hand." I love that this verse talks about falling down. So many times misinformed people try to convince us that the Christian lifestyle should be utopian, but God never promised that our lives would be perfect or that trials would never come our way. He did promise that when we fall down, He would be there to pick us up.

I have never heard of one single person who made it out of life completely unscathed. Challenges are a way of life, no matter if you are walking in God's favor or if you are a hopeless wreck. The only shame in being knocked down is staying there. Grab yourself by the bootstraps, stand up, and tell the enemy where he can go. You are more than a conqueror, so start acting like it!

When you are hit with news of an unexpected death, sudden loss, unemployment, or a tragic event you never anticipated, in an instant your existence is rocked to the very core. You are grasping at straws, trying to figure out where to turn.

Rest assured. God sees. He already knew about your storm before the first bolt of lightning struck. Will you allow Him to wrap His arms around you and carry you through the storm? Having a bad day doesn't mean that God has forsaken you or forgotten about you or that you are somehow insignificant. It doesn't mean that you aren't a real Christian or that your faith is weak. May I remind you of Jesus on the cross? The dark cloud lingering over Golgotha looked like the worst day in history, and yet the cross became a universal symbol of redemption for mankind.

Let's talk about some examples found in the Bible, with our old friends Sarah and Abraham. Their story highlights the very human side of Abraham, the side of him that thought he knew what was best for his own life. It is the great stuff of which novellas are made.

TRUST HIM AND KEEP HIKING UP THE MOUNTAIN

Abraham and Sarah, like so many of us, initially decided that their ideas were better than God's. Sarah was barren, so the two of them conspired together and decided that he should have a child with his wife's maid, Hagar. Being a wife myself, I can't say that I would have willingly signed on for this game plan let alone initiated the idea. But that's the way Sarah rolled. If I was writing this novella, Abraham would have been the recipient of a new residence, a butt-kicking right out of my tent for sure. Still, Hagar (the maid) became pregnant with Ishmael.

At this point Hagar became upset with Sarah (the nerve!) and decided to leave until an angel stopped her by a spring of water. The angel gave Hagar the baby's name, Ishmael, and told her that her son would be a wild man—just the news every new mother is looking to hear. Abraham was eighty-six when Ishmael was born.

A few years later God spoke to Abraham again at ninety-nine years of age. He said, "And I will make my covenant between Me and you, and will multiply you exceedingly" (Gen. 17:2). The Bible goes on to say that Abraham fell on his face and God told him that he would become the father of many nations. (This is when Abram's name was changed to Abraham, and Sarai became Sarah.)

I think I would fall on my face too if God told me I was going to multiply when I was one hundred years old! And even though Abraham laughed at the thought of having another child in his seemingly golden (more like platinum) years, God still blessed him with Isaac the following year.

Sometimes when shocking events happen in our lives, we don't know where to turn for help. Certainly having a baby at the age of one hundred would be shocking news for even the most prepared individual. But when God hands you an assignment, the best thing to do is buy the diapers and set up the crib, because the baby is on the way.

God gave Sarah and Abraham a gift when they least expected it. Isaac (which literally translates in Hebrew as "he laughs") came into their lives when they thought all hope of having a child of their own was lost, and God used him as a promise to bless the future generations of Israel, expanding Abraham's blessing to modern day. I would say that's one huge blessing.

Proving once and for all that laughter truly is the best medicine.

Going forward thirteen more years, Abraham became much wiser with age. Of course, one hundred years can certainly teach you a little about life. How many times have you told yourself, "If I only knew then what I know now"? Well, here is a snapshot of Abraham who had not only grown older but had also developed a deeper relationship with God. He no longer wanted to choose his own way, but he wanted to follow the path that led directly to God's will for his life. He had learned that God's way always leads to greater reward. And his faith carries him right up the mountain.

You can almost hear Abraham's footsteps as he trudged through the mountain range noted in Genesis as Mount Moriah (now known as the Temple Mount in Jerusalem, where Solomon built his temple). God wanted to see if Abraham would do what He asked, sacrifice what was most precious to him, the son he had waited an entire lifetime to conceive. You have to believe that Abraham would have given up anything else he owned (or would ever own in the future) for the opportunity to save his son. And still, he kept walking... one heavy foot in front of the other.

As Abraham continued to climb, he prayed and said, "God sees." Abraham had a heartbreaking dilemma on his hands. He was in a no-win situation. Does he sacrifice his son, or does he go against God's command?

Farther up the hill he continued to pray, "God sees." The fact that Abraham continued the upward climb, following God's command—even if he lost his son—is an unbelievable act of sheer faith. It is something you rarely see in human nature: complete surrender to God's will. As the altitude got higher and the air thinner, Abraham continued to lovingly lead his son by the hand.

The Bible notes that Isaac was old enough to walk beside Abraham, and some Talmudic studies say he was considered an adult at that point (at least thirteen years of age in the Hebrew culture). Think of the strong bond between father and son at that age. This was a child Abraham had desired for years; a son who had become the center of his universe was now what God was asking him to sacrifice. He was being asked to give up the very thing that meant the most to show his solidarity with God.

God saw and Abraham continued this death march, trusting in God even though he absolutely did not understand any part of this assignment or what good it could possibly bring. Oh, the pain that must have been coursing through Abraham's heart.

If God asked something like this of me, I would probably have to say, "Just strike me with a lightning bolt or do something to hurt *me*, not my kid." I honestly don't think I could do it. But still, Abraham kept hiking and saying, "God sees."

When father and son reached the very top of the mountain, Abraham began to prepare the altar. He bound Isaac and placed him on top. I cannot imagine the anguish. Abraham must have had all kinds of knots forming in his stomach and lumps in his throat. I can almost imagine him weeping as he carried out this extreme act of obedience. BUT GOD. Just as Abraham lifted his knife in the air over Isaac, an angel spoke to him. Abraham then looked over and saw a ram stuck in a bush. God let him know that the ram had been provided to take the place of his beloved son, and because of his faithfulness, the ram became the sacrifice. Isaac's life was spared.

You can almost see Abraham now weeping with joy at the sight of the ram, thanking God for His mercy. Abraham cried out to God and continued doing what he knew to be God's will for his life, even though he couldn't possibly see the tiniest thread of light at the end of the tunnel. From where Abraham stood, it must have looked like the worst possible scenario. But "God sees."

Know that this very same God (who is known across creation as the God of Abraham, Isaac, and Jacob) who saw this father's heart being torn to shreds can see your need. God sees. He is waiting to see if you will trust Him with the problem, with the heartache, with the reconciliation, with the solution.

Will you trust in Him and keep hiking up the mountain, one painful step at a time? If God clearly paints a line in the sand for you to follow, will you step up to the challenge and accept what He has in store for you, or will you go your own way?

I have said a prayer most of my adult life. "God, if there is someone whom I can help in any way, or whom I can tell about your goodness and mercy, please send them my way." Very simple but powerful. God has never failed to send people to me, right here at home. I don't have to be a jet-setter seeking out people with problems. They seem to find me pretty easily.

If God watches over the sparrows and paints the lilies in the valley, how much more important are we? God sees you no matter where you are. He knows your problem and the number of tears you have shed over it. He has the solution waiting for you. He is a master at fixing what we destroy. He heals. He restores. He sees.

Don't give up. God is able.

God's promises never fail. What He did for Abraham on Mt. Moriah, He can do for you. My prayer is that you will find some source of encouragement in this book for your own personal storm and have the courage to apply it to your own life. Be willing to open yourself up to unlimited success in every area of your life. Take the chance that you do actually deserve God's very best. Let the fear that dominated your life the moment you heard that fatal diagnosis, got fired from your job, or watched your spouse walk out dissipate. Replace that fear with the promise that you can do *all* things through Christ who strengthens you (Phil. 4:13).

Heavenly Father,

Our steps are ordered by You. Even though we may stumble and fall, You are sure to pick us up. You are the friend who sticks closer than any brother. Thank You for helping us trudge through every crazy mile of this lifetime and for loving us in spite of ourselves. Forgive us for the times we have fallen short, and help us to use these experiences to learn more about You. You are the God who sees. You see our needs and have the perfect solution before we know the problem even exists. Nothing is impossible with You, O God! We thank You for watching over us, and we place our future in Your capable hands. You are the same yesterday, today, and forever. What You have done for others, You can do for us. We ask that You surround us with Your mercy as we continue climbing up the mountain, not knowing what tomorrow holds. The beauty of this journey is that we know who holds tomorrow.

In Jesus's name, amen.

Chapter 10

GOD'S PERFECT PLAN

*"For My thoughts are not your thoughts, nor are
your ways My ways," says the Lord. "For as the
heavens are higher than the earth, so are My
ways higher than your ways, and My thoughts
than your thoughts. For as the rain comes down,
and the snow from heaven, and do not return
there, but water the earth, and make it bring
forth and bud, that it may give seed to the sower
and bread to the eater, so shall My word be that
goes forth from My mouth; it shall not return to
Me void, but it shall accomplish what I please, and
it shall prosper in the thing for which I sent it."*
—ISAIAH 55:8–11

I N JULY OF 2006 I was living in Houston, Texas, enjoying
refreshing summer showers and six weeks of radiation
at MD Anderson. My right leg had recently been oper-
ated on, which prohibited my driving, so various friends
and family members would stay with me during the week,
driving me back and forth to the hospital each morning.

On the weekends it was usually just my sweet daughter
Kassidee, who was only three years old at the time, and

me. We had great fun in our little condo, watching movies, walking across the street to go shopping, or just hanging out together. She was a living, breathing reminder of what I was fighting for. Her tiny smile was the very best part of my day.

One of my friends who came to stay with me was Linda Smith. Linda was in the middle of her own cancer treatments in San Antonio, and yet she took the time to drive up with Diana to see how I was doing. She was an amazing person, beautiful inside and out. I don't think I ever saw her (even in her chemo turban) without her best accessory—a constant smile from ear to ear.

Through numerous breast cancer recurrences, Linda put on her best red dress and painted the world with her smile. Even though she knew the odds were drastically stacked against her, she never doubted God's plan for her life. She didn't waste time on anger or fear but instead chose a path of forgiveness. Meeting with each family member and friend in her last days on earth, she lovingly made amends and passed from this life to the next.

Like all other funerals when a loved one is gone before we feel like it is their time to leave us, this was a sad celebration. On the one hand you knew she was pain free and dancing with the angels, long hair blowing in the breeze. On the other hand you looked at the pain on the faces of the children she left behind, and it drove a dagger deep inside your heart. She impacted the lives of many who gathered to honor her, a loving mother who celebrated each day and a living testimony of God's love.

I have, unfortunately, attended many funerals of friends

who have been taken by cancer. Each one is sad in its own way, but this one hit an all-time low.

As I was waiting with my family in the pew for the service to start, my husband, Jim, was in the church lobby being "let go" by his boss...after faithful service for almost four years. That screeching sound ringing in my ears during the service was our finances hitting a brick wall head-on. Questions flowed through my brain in an all-consuming flood of near panic.

It's one thing to face life's challenges when there is money in the bank, but it's a whole new ball game when the bank account runs dry. You can handle a lot of bad days if you don't have to worry about finances. I was afraid to ask what could possibly happen next on the hit parade. "I'll take 'Personal Tragedy' for $400, Alex."

Jim's boss was a friend, so it wasn't a matter of whether or not my husband was doing a good job. The work just wasn't there. The hard fact was that the construction industry had slowed to a limping crawl in San Antonio, and the accountant had advised Jim's boss to cut all business expenses— aka employees. It wasn't personal; it was business.

This didn't make the news any easier financially, but emotionally we knew there was nothing my husband could have done differently to save his job. My dad always says, "Some days you get the bear, and some days the bear gets you." This day was the bear's day.

I returned home from Linda's funeral, completely deflated. My emotional roller coaster of a day had left me feeling flatter than a piece of unleavened bread. I didn't think anything else could possibly make me feel worse. There was no silver lining in this particular rain cloud, only golf size hail pelting me from every angle. I was completely spent.

I would not know for several months exactly how this personal setback would end or where the lack of finances would take us, but God was faithful. There were times when throwing in the towel looked really good, but with each passing week I had to focus on the fact that we were that much closer to our answer, to the end of this incredibly trying slice of our journey. It wasn't pleasant, but God was faithful to give us exactly what we needed each day. I am someone who likes to plan ahead, so this was something that constantly weighed on my mind...wondering how my husband and I would be able to just meet the basic needs of our children. But we both made it a point to pray each day for direction and mercy, and it was a great lesson on faith that I have never forgotten.

NOT EVEN GENETICS CAN OVERRIDE GOD'S PERFECT PLAN

One of my very dear friends is married to a guy we will call Kyle. For more than thirty years Kyle struggled with the fact that his father was an alcoholic. Would Kyle turn into an alcoholic? If so, what would happen to his wife and two children? Everything he had worked so hard for could disappear in an instant. One wrong move could cause his life's work to come tumbling down.

Kyle had watched alcohol destroy his father's life, relationships, career, and marriage. He had seen the toll alcohol had taken on every member of his family. Kyle was careful to avoid celebrations where alcohol would be served, not trusting himself enough to even be around it. Though

Kyle had never had a drinking problem, he lived with the constant mental reminder of what alcohol could do when mishandled.

At the age of thirty-three, through the magic of Facebook, Kyle received a message that said, "I just wanted to let you know that I am your biological father. For circumstances I cannot explain in an e-mail, I had to give you up at birth. But I want you to know that I have never stopped loving you, and I hope you can forgive me for giving you up." It was the olive branch he never saw coming.

Suddenly years of fear and self-limitation melted away, and the enormous burden Kyle had been carrying since childhood evaporated in an instant, never to return. Soon after receiving this e-mail, Kyle went to physically meet his birth family. Today he has a second family and a new sense of self-confidence and freedom.

Sometimes it takes years for us to understand exactly what God's plan is for our life, but if we trust Him to lead us in the right direction, we are promised that He will bring us out to rich fulfillment. While sometimes the road we are on might take us along a somewhat circuitous route or to a place of great discomfort, when we have that "aha!" moment where God reveals what He was teaching us, it is worth every step it cost us to arrive at our divine destiny.

GRAB HOLD OF GOD'S GOODNESS

Sometimes God expresses His love for us in such a clear way that all we can do is sit back and say, "Thank You!" God's plan is an intricate display of His overwhelming love for us. His plans for our lives are bigger than our past, our family history, or any current personal issues that limit our success.

> And not only that, but we also glory in tribulations, knowing that tribulation produces perseverance; and perseverance, character; and character, hope. Now hope does not disappoint, because the love of God has been poured out in our hearts by the Holy Spirit who was given to us.
> —ROMANS 5:3–5

If you want to see God's perfect plan fulfilled in your own life, grab hold of the good things that come from the rain. Let the fire of life's circumstances purify you for whatever God has in store, knowing that He will supply all of your needs. No previous experience is required.

God has all power in heaven and on earth. Give Him thanks for the good things He has done in your life, and also for the battles that you face. You will soon find yourself on the winning side of your situation, standing victorious like David after his miraculous defeat over Goliath. And make sure that you, like David, give God the glory for your victory.

I love that God used someone with no previous giant-killing skills on his résumé, an unseasoned warrior. There couldn't have been anyone less qualified for this job than David. But God appointed him for this task and used David's willingness to bring blessings upon everyone around him.

What could we accomplish if we believed that anything we put our hand to would prosper? That *we* could be the giant killer? Would we continue dodging our problems, or would we face them head on with a mere slingshot?

Why do we often accomplish 2 percent of what we are actually capable of and shelve 98 percent of our potential? I believe we don't reach our full potential largely due to self-limitation and self-doubt. We have either convinced ourselves that we are incapable of reaching that mountaintop, or we have allowed someone else to tell us that we are too inept or simply don't deserve to attain such a lofty goal.

Maybe we are carrying around an emotional suitcase that we just need to unpack. Think of Kyle. We might not have even been carrying around our own baggage but borrowing from someone else's Samsonite filled with problems that don't even belong to us.

I live just outside of the city limits and often think of a young deer my children named Molly, who became our first neighbor. Many times I would open the door in the morning to leave for work, only to find Molly walking in my front door as quickly as possible, doing her subtle best to remind me that it was breakfast time. She had been waiting on the porch, and my dogs didn't begin to intimidate her. I literally had to shove her back out onto the porch and bring her a plate of food to keep her from heading straight for my living room. Nothing was going to deter Molly from her goal of starting her day right with a healthy breakfast.

She taught me a great lesson. No one had ever given Molly a manual on deer protocol. No one had ever told her that deer weren't supposed to go inside and search for breakfast, that she should be afraid of the unknown factors she might run into while searching through a stranger's home. So, Molly didn't wait outside with the other deer for breakfast to come to her; she went inside and made it happen for herself. Molly was smart enough to know that if I was bringing out platters of food, she was going to take a peek around and search for the source.

If she could have opened the fridge with her hooves, I'm sure she would have given it her best shot. She got the finest deer breakfast in the neighborhood each morning, because she was not afraid to go after what she wanted. She wasn't worried about listening to the herd, or what everyone else was doing, or if the other does were talking about her behind her back. ("Did you see how Molly just charged right in there?") She saw what she wanted and made a beeline for it without hesitation or apology. Molly lived a very fat and happy life until the day she died.

When I say that Molly didn't worry about what her deer friends thought, she just charged right in....am I being sarcastic? Absolutely! But the point is, you can't let people bring you down. Flawed humans that we are, we don't always celebrate the good things in the lives of our friends and family. Do not let that deter you from being thankful for your blessings or moving forward.

No one else's opinion should keep you from fulfilling God's unique plan for your life. The only opinion that should concern you is God's. He will take it up with your enemies when they mistreat you for following His will for your life. So get busy living! There is much to celebrate!

Heavenly Father,

Thank You that we are fearfully and wonderfully made, created in Your image for a purpose that no one else can fulfill. May we remember this when those around us would try to tear us down, when the enemy would send people to let us think less of ourselves. May we only seek Your approval. Lord, may we see ourselves as You see us. And may You give us a spirit of joy, peace, and love. May we not limit ourselves in our human thinking, but may we live a limitless life through Your Son.

In Jesus's name, amen.

Chapter 11

SHOULD YOU SHOOT THE MESSENGER?

Arise, go thy way: thy faith hath made thee whole.
—Luke 17:19, kjv

WHEN I WAS initially diagnosed with cancer, I received messages from two separate groups at the Wailing Wall (neither group was affiliated with the other in any way). My name was written on small strips of paper along with a prayer for my healing. In 2012 I celebrated being cancer free for five years, an incredibly savory milestone. As my parents were traveling to Israel that year, I asked them to please write my name on a new slip of paper, telling God thank you for my healing. It was the smallest act for the biggest favor.

Certainly God knew I was healed, but I wanted Him to be reminded of how very grateful I am for the gift of a second chance. I wanted the message of gratitude to resonate from one end of the globe to the other. I received many reassuring messages from God during my cancer journey, and the fact that my friends (without my asking) had taken the time to write my petition and place it in the Wailing Wall is something that I carry with me always. Some moments are so touching that they become a part of you.

But are all messages from God? How can you tell what/ who you should listen to? Messages come in all shapes and sizes, but how can you tell the difference between the wolf and the sheep? When someone tells you that they have a message from God for your life, what do you look for?

Many people wonder if the "voices" they are hearing inside their head are meant to guide them in the right direction or if they're just a nervous tic. I always think of the Disney movie *Pinocchio*, where the blue fairy tells Pinocchio, "Always let your conscience be your guide."* Actually, she wasn't too far off base. If we fill our life with the things of God, meditating on His Word, then the Holy Spirit sends us these messages that might feel like a still small voice in our spirit. But how do we know these messages are from God?

God's messages *always* line up with His Word and *never* sound like gossip or slander. These messages may come in the form of stern warnings but are never intended to tear someone down, only to build them up or encourage them in some way. Sometimes it isn't necessarily what we *want* to hear but what we *need* to hear. If we have spent time in the Word, it is easy to decipher if the message is from God because it will sound like a command found in Scripture, or maybe even a promise coming to fruition. God will *never* ask you to do something harmful to yourself or others, so weigh the message against the Word, and you will know right away if the message is discernment or indigestion.

In my own life I had one particularly annoying "saint" who consistently told me God was giving her messages

---

* IMDb.com, "Memorable Quotes for *Pinocchio*," http://www.imdb.com/title/ tt0032910/quotes (accessed February 28, 2013).

intended for me (and several others) that clearly did not line up with the Bible. She was a self-proclaimed prophetess who spread nothing but hatred and bitterness. Her messages were almost always delivered with an attitude of superiority and clearly outlined how God favored her and her perfection over the recipient of her message. She never had anything good to say, just messages about the wrongs that were committed by the offending party (the one to whom the message was being delivered).

When I was diagnosed with cancer, she said she would pray for me, even though she was certain I would lose my leg. She almost passed out when I asked her to please pray for anyone else *but* me. Fast-forward a few years (and a few more "prophecies" that were nothing more than a ploy for attention), and this healthy woman died in her sleep at a very young age. The first thing that came to my mind was Galatians 6:7: "Be not deceived; God is not mocked: for whatsoever a man soweth, that shall he also reap" (KJV).

If someone is telling you they have a message from God, be alert to the content of the message and the delivery style:

- Does this message clearly align with God's Word?

- Does it give you a positive, scriptural direction or declaration for your life?

- Does the message sound like it is coming from the flesh or the Spirit?

There is nothing better than an anointed word from God and nothing more destructive than someone who is self-appointed to spew personal venom and label it as a message from God.

If the person delivering the message exhibits a haughty, demeaning spirit, clearly this message is a personal vendetta and not from the Lord. Be vigilant, and start reading the Bible enough to know when God is using other people to speak to you and when Satan is trying to attack you by using other people. The old saying "Knowledge is power" is never truer than when you learn the promises found within the Word of God. You can use these promises as a shield of protection or as a guide to redemption. But the Word will never return void (Isa. 55:11).

If someone asks you to place them on your prayer list, this is a true honor. Taking someone else's needs before the throne is a huge responsibility, helping to carry their spiritual burden. Make sure that your own life is right with God before standing in the gap for someone else. And when you ask someone to return the favor, make sure those interceding on your behalf are praying according to Scripture and not their own personally manufactured beliefs.

James 5:16 says, "Pray one for another, that ye may be healed. The effectual fervent prayer of a righteous man availeth much" (KJV).

Let me give you a very powerful example of how the right message given in the right spirit can give you a spiritual breakthrough like none other.

One of my lifelong friends whom we will call Karo had felt in her spirit for several years that something was wrong with her two young daughters, ages nine and eleven. She had seen them go from upbeat, charismatic, outgoing young ladies to students whose grades were dropping and girls who were becoming more and more reclusive. The change was gradual over the last of their elementary school years, so Karo wondered if perhaps the changes were due to maturity and pending adolescence.

Karo had grown up in a Christian home, read the Word, attended church, prayed daily, and she had seen her fair share of crises. She knew firsthand the difference God could make in your life and knew the power of God that could be unleashed in any difficult situation.

As the months and years passed, she continued to pray blessings over her children and specifically prayed for their protection. Even so she continued to see the downward spiral in attitude and the deterioration of her children's self-esteem. She knew that something was wrong even though the girls continually told her they were fine.

One Sunday her pastor was teaching on the unmitigated power of God's blessing. At the end of the service Karo took her girls up to have the pastor pray a prayer of blessing over them, not thinking anything of it at all. I mean, who can't use an extra blessing in their life? The family went home, and there was no remarkable change to the human eye. But God was busy in heaven.

Matthew 16:19 says, "And I will give you the keys of the kingdom of heaven, and whatever you bind on earth will be bound in heaven, and whatever you loose on earth will be loosed in heaven."

Karo continued to pray, "God, please reveal to me what is happening to my children. Please make the unknown known." A few weeks passed, and her oldest daughter, Rene, attended a church camp. Again, nothing out of the ordinary, but the extraordinary took place when a twelve-year-old little girl stood up in front of the whole camp to share her testimony. Rene had seen her fair share of church events, but this was the first time she had attended a middle school retreat of any kind. This was a far cry from the elementary testimony of "Someone stole my backpack and God supplied me with a new one." This was the real, life-altering, lightning-striking deal.

As this incredibly brave twelve-year-old girl stood in front of more than two hundred peers, she began to relay the horrifying tale of an uncle who had abused her. She spoke of how her family had helped her through it once she had the courage to tell them and how God was healing her from the inside out. What this brave little girl didn't know was that my friend Karo's daughter was going through the very same thing... and no one had a clue. But God saw.

And He heard Karo's prayers. He heard the pastor's blessing. He sent the little girl to bring the right message at the exact time. A few days after returning from camp, Rene went to her mother and told her what had been happening in her own life.

Hearing that word from God gave her the courage to come forward after years of abuse. And God immediately set Rene free from bondage that very day. Two days later Rene's younger sister came forward with the same revelation. Though the pain was excruciating, the enemy had been revealed and the mother's prayers were answered—though certainly not in the way Karo expected. That one message delivered in the right spirit saved the lives of two little girls. To that brave twelve-year old who stood in front of a room full of friends and strangers, this book is dedicated.

Prayer makes a difference. It sets the captive free. It

binds Satan. It is, without a doubt, the most powerful tool you will ever have in your possession. Listen to what God is telling you, and act accordingly. Get rid of the false witnesses around you and get ready for the Holy Spirit to take you to a place of anointing, a place of limitless power through Jesus Christ.

Heavenly Father,

May we never forget to thank You! Prayer is a powerful gateway to the throne room, and we thank You for listening to each and every petition. Lord, when Satan sends a false messenger our way, make it plain for us to see. May we come to know You so intimately that the false words would burn our ears even as they are being spoken. We will know without a shadow of a doubt that the message is not from You. May these darts not penetrate the protective shield that we have formed for ourselves by speaking Your Holy Word out loud. Your Word is a light unto our path and also a light that uncovers words spoken deceitfully. Thank You for Your discernment and Your wisdom.

In Jesus's name, amen.

Chapter 12

PROBLEMS COME IN ALL
SHAPES AND SIZES

*I will repay you for the years the locusts have
eaten....You will have plenty to eat, until
you are full, and you will praise the name of
the Lord your God, who has worked wonders
for you; never again will my people be shamed.
Then you will know that I am in Israel, that I
am the Lord your God, and that there is no
other; never again will my people be shamed.*
—JOEL 2:25–27, NIV

I WAS AT MY children's elementary school one afternoon when I heard there were stranded kittens living in the woods behind the school's playground area. A huge animal lover, I had to assess the situation for myself. As I made my way to the wooded area, a flash of black fur dashed into the thick foliage so quickly that it was hard to follow.

By this time a crowd of elementary-age children had also received the stranded kitten memo and were all screaming and frantically waving their arms behind the chain-link fence separating the school from the woods. The clanging sound of the fence as they rocked back and forth was almost deafening. With this much activity I knew the kittens would never come out. I can't say that I blamed them.

I hiked up my skirt and jumped over the fence to see if I could get a better look. All I could see from my vantage point was the tiny black fur ball zipping from one hideout to the next. With all of the excitement emanating around the rowdy children, it was a lost cause. I climbed back over the fence in my heels and instructed the children to return to their dodge ball game. Being kids, they continued clinging to the fence and clanging as loudly as possible, as if their very lives depended upon the volume of the noise they created.

With a miniature circus coming to life behind the playground fence, I knew the kittens would run as far away as possible or dig in underneath the foliage. I started thinking of an alternate rescue plan because I knew within the next day or two we were expecting severe thunderstorms, making it impossible for the kittens to survive. They were living in an area that was geographically sloped downward, causing any rain to run off in their direction, literally flooding their temporary home. They also had no food, so time was of the essence.

After the school day was over and the playground was finally free of screaming children, I was ready to try again. I jumped back over the fence and stood completely still, waiting to see if anything would move. Sure enough, the black flash of fur was back. I waited and watched where he was going. No way could I catch him in heels, and no way were my shoes coming off in the woods. I love animals. Snakes? Not so much.

I had my girls join me in this expedition as they are well-seasoned animal rescuers. School was out, and I knew they would be thrilled at the thought of helping tiny kittens. My daughter Kassi was the first one I lifted over the fence. Once she walked to the rear exit of the wooded area, she froze and stood in complete silence, also waiting to see from which tree the black kitten would emerge.

My oldest daughter, Mckenzie, walked to the other side of the wooded area to block the exit to the street. We all realized that we were working against the clock. If other children noticed we were trying to catch the kittens, the circus would once again come to life.

We live in Texas, and the humidity was starting to pierce through my clothing; beads of sweat dripped down my back. Once I get hot, my patience starts to wear a little thin. So I was trying to make that rescue happen in a hurry.

Trudging through thick underbrush in my heels, I tried to gracefully squat down to see where the kitten was hiding. He was so tiny that if he didn't reveal himself, I would never find him. I was hot and uncomfortable while my girls were whispering that we could not give up. Praying that no one had a camera for the school yearbook, I looked into my daughter's ice blue eyes and knew that I had given her one of my best traits, sheer determination.

I finally spotted the kitten's home base and saw three tiny sets of eyes looking straight at me. At least I knew how many we needed to catch before calling it a day. The now familiar black fur ball sprinted to the other end of the woods, and I yelled for Kassi to grab him.

The gray kitten disappeared underground, and the black and gray tabby looked up at me with enormous green eyes as I scooped her up. She was precious but had no fight left in her. She was nothing but fur and bones covered in stickers and scrapes. Holding her tiny frame, I knew we simply could not leave the other two behind, no matter how much I was drenched in sweat. This glamorous rescue had to go on.

I handed the starving kitten over the fence to a teacher and went back for the other two. One blisteringly hot hour later I was able to finally catch the elusive black brother who was running as if his tail was on fire. He was faster than any Speedy Gonzales cartoon I have ever seen.

When Kassi and I were finally able to grab him, we saw that he too was covered with cuts and scrapes from living in the woods and fending for himself. There was no way he could be more than six weeks old. At that point I'm not sure which one of us looked worse, me or the scratched up fur ball. I'm pretty sure I resembled the melted version of the Wicked Witch of the West from *The Wizard of Oz* just before she evaporated.

Now I only had to find the third kitten, the gray one. And wouldn't you know? She darted down under the ground through a configuration of sheer rock. After another hour I was done. I didn't think anything could penetrate the exhaustion that had now settled over me, sweat and all. I was wrong. The sad look on my girls' faces shot an arrow right through my heart.

I told my girls we had done a great job, saving two of the three kittens. Now it was time to go home, make dinner, and pull the homework out of our backpacks. We would let the gray kitten calm down for a little while and come back for her later.

"Mom, you can't just save two kittens and leave the other one out there by herself."

"Mom, you will be responsible if that last kitten dies and you didn't try to save her."

I knew the weather forecast was not in our favor; the torrential downpour could strike at any moment. So I dropped the girls off at home, gently placing the kittens in a spare bedroom until I could take them to our vet, Dr. Corder. Dr. Corder is really an angel among us. He has helped us over the years with too many animals to count, so I knew he would be happy to help save these tiny rescues.

I fed the girls and then ran upstairs to feed the kittens before heading back to the school. As soon as I put the plate of food down in front of the two kittens, they ate like it was the last morsel of food they would ever see. They couldn't get it in fast enough.

They were so malnourished they didn't even stop to smell what they were eating, which is very unusual for cats. Without a word I changed into my jeans and drove back to the school to find the gray sister.

I will give her this; she was not going down without a fight. I had to admire her tenacity. It took more than an hour to hunt her down, as she kept bobbing in and out of holes in the ground and dense foliage. I was not about to lose my arm by sticking it down some dark hole in the woods, but I knew that my persistence would pay off eventually. I was praying that I didn't drown in the humidity before finding the elusive gray sister. The air was like hot soup.

When I finally put my hand around this tiny lump of gray and felt how emaciated she was, I knew I had done the right thing. And since no good deed goes unpunished, as I wrapped my fingers around her frame to secure her from hurting herself, she sank her teeth into my thumb as if she were competing in the bite mark Olympics. I refused to let go because I knew that this single act would save her life.

The point is that sometimes we need a little rain to motivate us to get moving. If it wasn't for the rain, I probably would have delayed saving the kittens. Perhaps they would have died before I found all of them.

I love the lessons animals teach us. The black brother was willing to run around in circles in order to avoid the unknown. He had no way of knowing if I was friend or foe, but even though he was living a life saturated in lack, he didn't want to venture outside his comfort zone. He was content with living in squalor and literally starving to death.

The striped sister didn't care one way or the other. She was simply exhausted and starving. The gray sister didn't want any part of it and was ready to fight to the end. She was willing to risk her life by running into underground caverns rather than move to a new environment. She didn't want to trade "better" for "best."

God is telling us that we need to trust Him to take us to a place in our lives where all of our needs will be met. He is willing and able to rescue us if given the opportunity, but He does not force His blessings on anyone. We need to be willing to let go of what is in our hand in order to trade it for what is in God's.

There are many things in life that require rain to grow. While too much rain can be challenging, it presents the choice to either seek shelter (God) or drown. If you are thinking that you could do with a little less rain in your life, consider what a good amount of pressure does to a lump of coal. Would you prefer to be chalky like coal or as stunningly brilliant as a priceless diamond?

Sometimes we have life-threatening problems, and sometimes we have hang-nail type problems we can fix on our own (like a flat tire). If you don't have the funds to pay for the flat tire, ask God to intervene on your behalf to make a way. If you have the funds and are fully capable, then just make it happen. Stop complaining about the bad day you're having, and just buy a new tire. The sky is not falling, Chicken Little.

If someone else has a need and you can fulfill it, you don't need to pray about it; just help them.

God is willing to provide for all of our needs according to His riches in glory. He has promised to not only provide for our needs that arise on a daily basis but also to restore that which Satan has tried to destroy. We need only to be still (Exod. 14:14).

One of my favorite Scripture passages is Psalm 3:1, 3, which says, "LORD, how they have increased who trouble me! Many are they who rise up against me.... But You, O LORD, are a shield for me, my glory and the One who lifts up my head." Sometimes you feel like bullets are raining down on every side of your life. Shots are being fired from every angle. Anger. Bitterness. Unforgiveness. Hatred. Poverty. Rejection. Mistrust. Fear. Regret. Sadness.

None of these things are from God, but He can certainly shield you from every obstacle and deflect every bullet meant to harm you. As a child I would picture God like Wonder Woman with her awesome bullet-deflecting golden bracelets. As an adult I realize that God can do this and so much more . . . even without the bracelets.

You don't have to continue living in the deep underbrush of the woods because it's the only way of life you've ever known. Reach for the Son, and find out what real living is all about. Dare to give up what you have to obtain something better. Rejoice in the great hope we have through Jesus Christ!

Romans 5:3–4 says, "We also glory in tribulations, knowing that tribulation produces perseverance; and perseverance, character; and character, hope."

Bring on the rain. With God on your side you *cannot* lose.

I understand that trust is a hard thing to do, but it is an essential key to walking with the Lord. We never know what will happen in our lives from one day to the next. We remain completely focused on this tiny little picture frame we are operating within for this brief second of our existence, a veritable snapshot of our lives. We need to focus on the bigger picture, on the overall plan God has for us. We need to know that there is something better waiting for us if we will only trust and obey.

Heavenly Father,

Let us learn how to be still, how to fully trust You with our problems. Let us know that when faced with an impossible situation, we can turn to You for the answer, knowing that heaven will send its very best just for us. We do not have to be stuck in our comfort zone. You can gift wrap an answer that we could never have come up with on our own. Please take away any sadness, bitterness, anger, or unforgiveness in our lives. Your Word says that if we don't forgive others, You cannot forgive us. We don't want anything standing in our way. We do not choose to live with regret. We stand up today and say that we are more than conquerors through Christ Jesus!

In Jesus's name, amen.

Chapter 13

DIVINE FAVOR

*I will extol thee, O Lord; for thou hast lifted me
up, and hast not made my foes to rejoice over me.
O Lord my God, I cried unto thee, and thou hast
healed me. O Lord, thou hast brought up my soul
from the grave: thou hast kept me alive, that I
should not go down to the pit. Sing unto the Lord,
O ye saints of his, and give thanks at the remem-
brance of his holiness. For his anger endureth
but a moment; in his favour is life: weeping may
endure for a night, but joy cometh in the morning.*
—PSALM 30:1–5, KJV

MY OLDEST DAUGHTER, Mckenzie, has attended the same school since she was four. Many of the children she has known since day care. So we knew that something serious had gone down at school when she announced, at the tender age of nine, that she didn't want to return—ever. Evidently her teacher was leaving the classroom and going to work with her husband in their family-owned business. Logically I can understand why an adult might not want to spend her entire day in a room with small, unrelenting children who never stop talking or moving during their waking moments, but my daughter, on the other hand, did not.

Mckenzie does not deal well with change, and she took her teacher's leaving very personally. "Why doesn't our teacher want to be with us any more?" I began explaining that her teacher's leaving was not personal. She was not leaving because of some offense perpetrated by the little minions in her charge. Life is too short to not enjoy it by doing all that you can to make each day count. All of my educated brilliance could not come up with an acceptable explanation as to why her teacher was leaving. Mckenzie wasn't buying it.

I told her we should pray together that God would place her in a new class with the perfect teacher to meet her individual needs. I tucked her tightly into bed and we prayed together, setting the example of what she needs to do in a time of crisis. Then I returned to my own room and prayed by myself, knowing that my child's sense of security was crushed. She felt like her universe was crumbling down around her. From her perspective this was a monumental shift in the paradigm of life.

Dear God,

I place my child's education and happiness before You. No matter how small or how great the problem, You promised that You would always inter-cede on our behalf. I'm asking that right now You give Mckenzie total peace, total confidence in who she is. I'm asking You to bless her in her going out and her coming in, to send Your angels to go before her and to be her rear guard. I ask that You defeat

her enemies and that You make her path straight.
Please guard her precious heart as she moves to a
new class, and place her exactly where You would
have her. Give her a teacher who has a heart for
You and the patience of a saint. Let Mckenzie con-
tinue to grow in the strength and knowledge of You,
and do not make this a stumbling block to her edu-
cation. Let her grow in wisdom and stature, and
may her days be those of heaven on earth. I thank
You for the answer that is already on the way.
Amen.

I would love to say that the moment this prayer was uttered it was smooth sailing, but that would be like saying the *Titanic* encountered a little turbulence. The third-grade waters were choppy for a while as Mckenzie anticipated moving to her new class with the zeal of someone being taken in front of a firing squad. There were several nights of long talks centered around the exhaustive topic, "I'm sure it will get better." A few weeks later it finally did.

My daughter was placed with a precious lady who is a pastor's wife and has the patience of Job. Mrs. Mendez has the gentlest spirit, maintaining a calm demeanor while slugging it out in the trenches. I can't say that if you stuck me in a room loaded with eighteen high-octane kids, I would be anything resembling gracious. I would probably be wishing I could use a very large roll of duct tape without going to jail.

But she handled the transition of gaining extra students into her room with regal poise and grace. She made the rest of Mckenzie's year even better than the beginning, and before long (much to my relief) Mckenzie had put her plans of quitting school aside. Mrs. Mendez was the perfect answer to our prayer.

A Mother's Day Triumph

By May Mckenzie was fully entrenched in her new third-grade class, and I was invited to attend a Mother's Day tea hosted by her teacher. When I walked into the classroom, I was crushed by the overwhelming reminder of how unbelievably merciful God is. I was walking into a room that I would have never seen if cancer had won. I was spending this moment in time with my daughter, who could have easily attended my funeral just a few short years ago. The gravity of the moment took me by surprise, and a flood of gratitude began to pour over me as if I had just heard the words "cancer free" yesterday.

I sat down in the tiny blue plastic chair by Mckenzie's desk and did my best not to sob uncontrollably as this stark realization hit. What Satan had meant for evil, what he had meant for my ultimate destruction, God had continued to use for His good. I couldn't help but think of the Cross. O death, where is your sting?

Before long, as I began recounting the many blessings in my life, my emotions got the best of me. The full impact of this day hit me like ice water in the desert. Silent tears of gratitude were streaming down my face as I gazed over the bulletin board featuring the hand-drawn pictures of all the classroom mothers. Each child had drawn a depiction of how they see their mom. I immediately knew which one Mckenzie had drawn before I even saw her name...and not just because I was the only mom in the room with red hair.

She had painstakingly drawn every feature of an outfit I have in my closet and made sure I was wearing the perfect accessories. It looked as if I had sat for the portrait.

This was Mother's Day, one of many days Satan tried to steal from me. Sitting next to me was a girl who could have very easily grown up without a mother. Without *me*. How can you thank God enough for giving you more time with your kids? How can you thank Him enough for sparing your life?

I was almost able to not publicly humiliate my daughter by barely containing my tears, when she proudly handed me a pink cardboard plaque she had made in the computer lab. This beautiful piece of artwork said:

M—Most Beautiful

O—Observant

T—The Best Mother Ever

H—Hard Worker

E—Exciting

R—Really Sweet

By this time my makeup was melting right down my chin and spilling onto my neck. I was giving Tammy Faye a real run for her money. I tried to laugh through my tears to lighten the moment. When I saw the word *exciting*, all I could think of was, "Her idea of exciting and mine are *totally* different."

I wanted to stand up and scream from the rooftop of the school, "Take that, Satan! You tried to destroy me. You tried to make me miss this perfect day. You tried to steal my future, and you failed miserably!" Every positive emotion I had ever felt was running through my body all at once. I was still here to share that precious day with my daughter. It just doesn't get any better than that!

I was lost in my own thoughts when Mrs. Mendez invited everyone to come to the dessert table for cookies and punch. Since I had been sick for the two days before the tea, I told Mckenzie to just get enough for herself. She understood, but I'm sure she was wondering why I was sitting there in a tiny chair (feeling like Gulliver—a huge person in a tiny seat), hugging her in a vice grip and crying as if I had to fill up the Guadalupe River with my own tears. Poor thing. She was a real trooper, brown spiral curls bouncing as she filled up a tiny paper plate with snacks for one.

I had once again regained minimal composure when the teacher invited me to move to a chair in the front of the room where Mckenzie was told to read the original Mother's Day letter she had written for me. All eyes in the classroom were on me and my raccoon eyes. I only wished I was at the little Mexican restaurant where I could place my miniature white flag in the down position. Check, please.

How could I sit in front of Mckenzie's classmates and their moms and not *completely* embarrass my child? How could I explain God's overwhelming goodness, favor, mercy, and love?

I held my breath and sat in the chair selected for me as every eye in the room focused on Mckenzie reading her special Mother's Day letter. All I could think of was, "I will not cry. I will not cry. I will not embarrass my daughter any more than I already have. I will not cry."

I'm not afraid of crowds or being in front of people, no

matter if it's ten or ten million. I was just doing my best to keep my daughter from disowning me before the end of the school day. I could already hear her telling a therapist, "There was this time in third grade..."

As I continued to fight a losing battle with the tear factory, Mckenzie began reading her poem aloud to this small gathering of classmates she had grown up with and their mothers. I only thought I was crying before.

> *Dear Mom,*
>
> *You are smart, beautiful, and talented. When I have trouble on my homework, you help me because you are so smart. I like the way you start singing to songs on the radio because you can sing so beautifully. I love when you smile, and it makes me happy when you laugh. I like to try to make you laugh if you are upset because you have a wonderful smile! I love to go shopping after school with you all the time and eat your favorite food, spaghetti. You always buy us new clothes when we grow out of ours. You are always fun to be around! There are a hundred words to call you and they are all wonderful. You are the best mom in the whole wide world!*
>
> *Love,*
> *Mckenzie*

That, my friends, is the cherry on top of the ice cream sundae that is *total* victory! To God be the glory, for great things *He* has done.

FAVOR FROM THE PIT TO THE PALACE

It is an amazing conundrum how quickly things can change from sunshine beaming through every possible crack of your life to living in the middle of a black storm cloud. By the time I was driving home from this amazing Mother's Day tea, my upset stomach had turned into a full-fledged virus with a raging fury. I didn't even make it home before I started vomiting uncontrollably. Not my finest hour.

As soon as I made it to the welcome sight of my driveway, I turned off the motor and ran inside to jump in the shower. No hot water. I got out and took my clothes to the washroom. The clothes washer wouldn't turn on. By this time I was turning green and doing my best to crawl to bed for some sweet relief.

On the way to my room I quickly considered announcing that we wouldn't be wearing clothes for a while until I figured out what was wrong with the washer. Just as quickly I realized my younger daughter, Kassi, might like that idea. Scratch that one. I pulled the covers up over my head and hoped it would make everyone disappear for a while.

It was a long night, but by morning I was feeling much better. It was time to put on my best insincere smile and give my husband the good news about our washer croaking. The words weren't even out of my mouth when he interrupted to tell me that our mattress had cracked in half with age and needed to be replaced.

Within five minutes I saw the washer in pieces, spread out all over the laundry room floor. My husband was fighting back his own frustration to fix the aging appliance that in any society would be deemed a relic. At that moment of complete household chaos I thought of the many people who had stopped me over the years to tell me they would love to have my perfect, glamorous life. I could not stop laughing.

In my life I don't think there are any light drizzles. It's usually a full-blown storm with lightning striking anything that dares to move. But how refreshing rain can be when you see the beauty behind the rainbow.

Living in God's favor does not mean your life will be easy or full of nonstop fun. Favor means that you have a friend to guide you through the storm to the gift that awaits you on the other side of the raging water. He is there to bring the lifeboat around when you feel like you are drowning.

With the favor of God you can overcome *any* bad day.

Life is about choices. We don't always make the perfect choices, but fortunately we serve a forgiving God who is deeply concerned with our well-being. TODAY is the day to make a difference. It is the day to put on your big boy or big girl pants and come to the realization that Christ's redemption was a priceless gift available to everyone...even you. Look at the bigger picture of what your life could become and start trusting in the infallible truths found in the Word of God. You will *never* go wrong by trusting in a God who cannot fail you.

In our shortsighted mind-set we have a hard time trusting anyone with our future until we actually see it unfold. It's the old saying about hindsight being 20/20. Oftentimes we are the tiny fly looking at just one piece of the artwork, maybe a portion that has been painted in a deep, flat black pattern. This portion looks very bleak. However, if you pull back and see the bigger picture, you notice that in fact the sea of black you were previously surrounded by is a beautiful masterpiece where many shades work together to illustrate the whole story.

Can you imagine being Joseph? Talk about a lot of black

spots on your tapestry. At the age of about seventeen God gave him two dreams, both of which showed his brothers bowing down to him. When he told his brothers, they were not big fans. Shocker! They took him out one day and threw him in a pit, beautiful coat and all.

The Bible records in Genesis that Joseph was the first son of Rachel and Jacob, and (even though there were eleven others who shared the same father) he was Jacob's favorite. The coat, the favoritism, and the dreams landed Joseph in a bit of a tight spot. If you think your family is dysfunctional, you should read the full story in Genesis. The antics of this group would make a great HBO special.

If I were Joseph, right about the time I was being shoved into the pit, I might have been thinking, "God, was that *You* telling me everyone was going to bow in front of me, or were the late-night spicy nachos not a good snack idea? After all, last night I was in my own comfy bed; tonight I'm enjoying a mud mat. Did I misunderstand what You were trying to tell me? Did I misinterpret the dream?"

We all know that Joseph's incredibly trying journey from the pit to the palace led him to a place where he eventually became the most powerful ruler in the world. Eventually. First the brothers took Joseph from the pit and sold him into slavery, spreading goat's blood on his beautiful coat. Jacob, believing Joseph was dead, mourned the loss of his beloved son.

As a slave Joseph ended up as a servant to Potiphar's wife. Potiphar was the captain of Pharaoh's guard and a very powerful man in Egypt. Joseph soon became the manager of Potiphar's household affairs until his wife wanted to have one of her own. When Joseph refused to have an affair with Potiphar's wife, she cried rape. For this, Joseph was rewarded with a jail sentence.

After he spent some time in jail, he gained the favor of the warden and was put in charge of the other inmates. Soon the chief baker and the chief cupbearer were sent to prison, right next to Joseph. They both had dreams that they asked Joseph to interpret. The dreams meant that the chief cupbearer would be reinstated, but the chief baker would be hanged. When the cupbearer was reinstated, Joseph asked him to please remember him, to put in a good word for him with Pharaoh.

Two years passed. No one remembered that Joseph was still in prison for a crime he never committed. Now it was time for Pharaoh to have a dream. This was his famous dream about seven lean years of famine and seven years of great harvest. Joseph (even though he had been ridiculed and stomped on in the past for his interpretations) went out on a limb one more time and told Pharaoh that he should start storing grain for the famine to come. Pharaoh released Joseph from prison and put him in charge of all Egypt, even adorning him with his signet ring and fine clothing.

And, of course, the grand finale (fireworks and theme music please). Joseph's brothers showed up front and center at the palace looking for grain to feed their families and livestock. You can almost hear the thoughts running through his mind.

If he were like many of us, he would have been plotting his revenge for years while trapped in a prison cell, just waiting for the moment he could repay his brothers for their multiple transgressions. But not Joseph. He never allowed bitterness or anger to overtake him. He never allowed them to steal his joy or take God's favor from him.

Genesis 45:4–8 says:

> I am Joseph your brother, whom you sold into Egypt. But now, do not therefore be grieved nor angry with yourselves because you sold me here; for God sent me before you to preserve life. For these two years the famine has been in the land, and there are still five years in which there will be neither plowing nor harvesting. And God sent me before you to preserve a posterity for you in the earth, and to save your lives by a great deliverance. So now it was not you who sent me here, but God; and He has made me a father to Pharaoh, and lord of all his house, and a ruler throughout all the land of Egypt.

Joseph saw the bigger picture. Instead of reliving every painful detail of his past, he shared the great prosperity of the country with those who had hurt him the most. When Joseph became the ruler of all Egypt, it had been more than twenty years since he had worn a beautiful robe. And yet the Bible records that Joseph *never* lost favor with God. No matter how many difficult situations he struggled through, God was *always* with him. And if you look closely at Joseph's story, he also held favor with man (Ps. 30:5).

From the outside it may not have looked like Joseph was living a favored life, just sitting around eating bon bons in the lap of luxury. However, when Joseph was in prison, he was placed in charge of the other prisoners. When he was a slave, he ran the entire household. These might not have been lofty positions and may have looked like the bleak, black dots of a canvas, but when the canvas was complete, it was a beautiful picture. Joseph made a choice to serve God, even when things looked bad.

Sometimes God takes us on a winding journey we could never have imagined to mold us into something beautiful, bringing us to a place far greater than we could have prepared on our own (Ps. 66:8–12). Favor doesn't always mean things go 100 percent our way. It means that God protects us through the worst of times.

If God can create the generational promise of a rainbow, close the mouths of hungry lions, and hand out palace-style promotions, I think you should be able to trust Him with your job search or the anger you are harboring for your neighbor who watered his lawn on the wrong day. There is no problem too great or too small (Jer. 33:3). Simply trust in Him, and get ready to walk in divine favor!

Heavenly Father,

When we look around us, on our darkest day, we are drowning in Your favor. We are blessed and highly favored, certainly blessed beyond our deserving. Nothing we could have ever done could earn the blessings You have freely given us. We ask that You use us, like Joseph, in a mighty way. May we face our trials with grace and have the attitude of gratitude. May we praise You in all things, even when trapped inside the most difficult of circumstances. May Your favor abound in our lives, and may all who see us know that You alone are our source.

In Jesus's name, amen.

Chapter 14

PRAY LIKE YOU MEAN IT

*Then you will call upon Me and go and
pray to Me, and I will listen to you. And
you will seek Me and find Me, when you
search for Me with all your heart.*
—Jeremiah 29:12–13

IF YOU HAVE a toolbox at your house, you know there are tools and there are power tools. This is the difference between taking your handsaw out to the front yard and spending several days cutting down a tree, and just firing up the motor to your electric saw and yelling "timber" in a matter of minutes.

If you are looking to cut through the forest of circumstances that is surrounding you, blocking you from the Son, there is no greater power tool in your arsenal than prayer. If you are not practiced in the art of prayer, there is no better time to start than right now. You can build a strong relationship with Jesus Christ by utilizing this one tool, unleashing power that can instantaneously revolutionize your life.

> Then He called His twelve disciples together and gave them power and authority over all demons, and to cure diseases. He sent them to preach the kingdom of God and to heal the sick.
>
> —LUKE 9:1–2

> And I will give you the keys of the kingdom of heaven, and whatever you bind on earth will be bound in heaven, and whatever you loose on earth will be bound in heaven.
>
> —MATTHEW 16:19

These verses clearly give us the ability to have power over all evil things through Jesus Christ. The initiative lies with us. Are we going to ask God for healing? Will we cast out demons or bind curses in His name? All of this supernatural power is available to us today, but will we utilize this power tool or simply leave it hanging in our garage?

He has promised in His Word to give us the authority we need to conquer those things that concern us most. God is just waiting for us to build a close enough relationship with Him that we don't have to guess what He means. When we hear His voice, we recognize it and follow the directions we are given. When we use this sacred authority, we release unlimited blessing and favor upon our lives.

Do you talk with God frequently enough to have a genuine relationship with Him? When you phone a friend, do you just say, "Hey! What's up?" Or do you have to say, "Hey, Sally! This is Sue. Remember me? We were friends in the third grade." Is your voice recognizable, or do you have to identify yourself and your reason for calling? If you are good friends, you probably just say hello and dive right into the conversation. No formalities or introductions are needed between close friends.

You want to have a relationship with God like He is your best friend. When you cry out to Him in the midnight hour, you want the assurance that the perfect solution is already on the way and that good things are about to happen.

Like every other part of the Christian life, there are guidelines to follow regarding effective prayer (James 5:16).

I think it is our natural instinct as human beings to ask people their opinion. And there is nothing wrong with asking the right people for their opinions. The Bible says to seek out the elders for their wisdom and glean from their knowledge. Somehow this has morphed into asking people to "pray about it" while spreading it down the gossip chain. There is nothing about this act of "prayer" that glorifies God in any way. So before you ask someone to "pray about it," make sure your intentions are sincere, and only ask people to pray for things that directly relate to you and your family.

Also, take into account the character of the person you are asking to pray for you. I'm not saying that if they aren't Jesus Christ or one of the disciples they can't pray for you, but what does their own moral compass look like? Do they follow the commands found in the Bible? Do they understand what it means to stand in the gap for a fellow believer? If they cannot pray for you and believe with 100 percent faith that God has the ability to meet your need according to *His* will, don't ask them to pray for you.

I don't want someone who took a chemistry class in tenth grade to operate on my failing heart. I want a real surgeon, someone who went a little further than a high school lab. It is the same when you are asking someone to pray for you. You want someone with experience, someone who knows the God of Abraham, Isaac, and Jacob and believes that God is still on the throne, making miracles happen every day. If you are ready to move mountains, don't couple yourself with someone who is still caught up in the minutia of the molehill.

Here is a story of a family who prayed for God's direction concerning receiving orphans into their home.

GOD WILL MAKE A WAY

My dad was the pastor of a small church in San Antonio, Texas. Of course, being a pastor means dealing with both good and bad, baptisms and funerals. Today was funeral day...and it was three days before Christmas. *¡Feliz Navidad!*

As he gathered the small crowd around the grandmother's casket, he looked around to see the expressions on the faces of those in attendance. Unlike other larger crowds he had preached to, this crowd was not only small but also very young. There were three young boys and their schoolteachers.

After the service one teacher told the pastor that the boys had been left at an orphanage in Ohio, each having different fathers. They had not seen their mother since the day she dropped them off, and there were no other known relatives. When the grandmother (the deceased) discovered the boys were abandoned, she brought them to her home in Texas. Now she was gone. What would become of these young boys who were clearly unable to care for themselves?

Having lived with their diabetic grandmother for seven

years, the boys knew their options were slim and none. The odds were clearly stacked against them. Even at eight, nine, and ten years of age, as they huddled together to pay their final respects, the youngest voiced what everyone was thinking. "*Now* what are we going to do?" He had found his grandmother lying lifeless on the living room couch just days before and felt the very small fragment of stability slipping quickly through his tiny fingers. Clearly life had dealt them a harsh blow at a very impressionable age.

The pastor met with another family in the church to see if they would be interested in adopting the three boys. Unfortunately this did not work out for them as they had recently lost a son in a farming accident and weren't emotionally ready to add to their family. Having worked in an orphanage as a teenager, the pastor knew what the future held for them if they were awarded to the state on a permanent basis. He could not give up on these boys.

After several intense conversations with God, the pastor decided, "If You are bringing these boys into our lives, You will make a way."

With this proclamation, and acting on blind faith, the pastor's family welcomed the three young boys into their modest home with open arms. They didn't have the funds to double their family size overnight, but they were willing to obey God when he sent them a challenge that seemed impossible.

James 1:27 says, "Pure and undefiled religion before God and the Father is this: to visit orphans and widows in their trouble, and to keep oneself unspotted from the world."

As the boys walked into their new home, they carried all of their earthly possessions in a small, wrinkled, brown paper bag. Not one bag per boy, but one single bag. The clothes on their backs were so tattered and torn that they were immediately discarded.

The boys had a new permanent home, and the future looked incredibly bright from their limited vantage point. They couldn't see the financial strain or the fact that they weren't living in a mansion. They didn't care. They were no longer concerned about being sent to an orphanage or separated between multiple families. Their story wouldn't end with their grandmother's death. This was just the beginning.

Of course, like any tight-knit group, the church was instantly flooded with the news of the latest arrivals. The church community began to donate materials and supplies to enclose their carport. Carpenters and weekend warriors stepped up to do the work free of charge. In no time at all, the carport was transformed into a fully enclosed, wood-paneled, lush-carpeted bedroom, complete with two wooden bunk beds and all the accessories necessary to house three growing boys. Various pieces of furniture were donated, and the walls were coated with soft blue paint.

A church member who was a buyer for a local department store took the boys shopping for new clothes. What once was contained in a tiny paper sack now filled up an entire closet to overflowing. Another church member owned a grocery store and donated fresh fruits, meats, and vegetables each week.

From any earthly perspective, there was no way this young pastor's family could have supported these three boys who so desperately needed a place to call home. Yet they felt God had placed them in the right spot at the right time.

There were numerous practical reasons why this humanitarian effort should *never* have worked. They didn't have the tools necessary to put God's plan into action. They didn't have the money or the space. They didn't have enough food to feed extra family members. No matter how deep their desire to help, this family was not capable of single-handedly taking on this daunting task. But when God gave them the instruction to help these boys, they moved them right in. They didn't stop and make excuses about how difficult it would be or wait for God to tell them every piece of the plan. They simply obeyed God, and He blessed them abundantly. This family lacked for nothing, and these boys became part of a home they desperately needed.

God didn't just stop with the big-ticket items like lodging and food. There was no need that wasn't met. And with children there are always plenty of needs: glasses, dental work, surgeries, counseling, special education for dyslexia. Each need was turned over to God, and mountains were moved.

After three years an uncle returned from the US Navy and invited the boys to move in with him. And, just that fast, another new chapter started for the boys. At four years of age I stood in the doorway of my house and waved good-bye to my three foster brothers. It would be several years before I would see them again, but I have never doubted that God has always held them right in the palm of His hand.

PRAYER 101

There is more to prayer than just sending up a divine order, telling God how and when you expect Him to meet your needs. Prayer is about asking and *listening*. It's about reception and not humanistic perception.

If we are interested in truly hearing from God, all we have to do is ask (Jer. 33:3). The Bible is very clear on how to pray, when to pray, where to pray, and what to expect. If you want an answer from above, the Lord's Prayer is the ultimate example. It's a simple template for Prayer 101.

> And when thou prayest, thou shalt not be as the hypocrites are: for they love to pray standing in the synagogues and in the corners of the streets, that they may be seen of men. Verily I say unto you, They have their reward. But thou, when thou prayest, enter into thy closet, and when thou hast shut thy door, pray to thy Father which is in secret; and thy Father which seeth in secret shall reward thee openly. But when ye pray, use not vain repetitions, as the heathen do: for they think that they shall be heard for their much speaking. Be not ye therefore like unto them: for your Father knoweth what things ye have need of, before ye ask him. After this manner therefore pray ye: Our Father which art in heaven, Hallowed be thy name. Thy kingdom come. Thy will be done in earth, as it is in heaven. Give us this day our daily bread. And forgive us our debts, as we forgive our debtors. And lead us not into temptation, but deliver us from evil: for thine is the kingdom, and the power, and the glory, for ever. Amen.
>
> —MATTHEW 6:5–12, KJV

Where do you pray? In private, an intimate moment between you and God. Yes, there are times for corporate prayer, and you can certainly cry out for help in a crowd. But God's idea of prayer is a very personal interaction between the two of you. Prayer is not something done for show so that everyone around you can know how "spiritual" you are.

If you need an audience to say a prayer so they can be amazed by your fantastic prayer verbiage, something so "holy" that they need to be a Shakespearean expert to understand...you might want to read the breakdown in the Bible. God doesn't say, "Gather a crowd around you; talk as loudly as you can in a firm voice so that you can impress people with what you say." God says that prayer is about Him, not you. It is about giving Him the opportunity to meet your need and giving Him the glory for the victory. Prayer is not about garnering attention for yourself.

The Bible clearly says that when you go to Him, He will meet your needs for all to see. This will be done openly. Why does God reward so publicly? He wants to see if you will give *Him* the honor and tell others of His wondrous works. He wants to know if you will take the glory for yourself ("WOW! I must be *some* kind of prayer warrior!") or if you will point toward the heavens and say, "My Redeemer lives! It is through Him and in Him that I have my being. He is the One who heard my cry and answered my prayer. He delivered me from the tempest."

Deuteronomy 6:11 says that He will give you houses you didn't build and vineyards you didn't plant. In case you aren't interested in the vineyards, take a different approach. Do you need healing? God is not only able to heal you, but

He is able to restore you—physically, emotionally, spiritually, on every possible level (Joel 2:25).

Do you need financial gain? He owns the cattle on a thousand hills (Ps. 50:10). Is your marriage crumbling? He will restore to you what the locusts have eaten (Joel 2:25), that which Satan has destroyed in your life.

Once you pray and ask God for something, get ready to receive the answer. As I said before, you need to be receptive to what God has in store for you. This may not mirror your own plans, but God's will is always perfect if you allow Him to complete it without interruption or deviation. The detours in our lives are not God's ideas; they typically come from our own foolish choices. (Welcome home, prodigal son!)

There is no questioning when God gives you a clear message, but you must be open to hearing it without editing it. You need to receive the message, knowing your current perception of where you are going might not be what God has in store for your future. Your perception is not always God's reality. If what you perceive to be the truth doesn't line up with God's Word, then your perception is wrong.

Prayer is a direct lifeline to God the Father. There is no call waiting or straight-to-voicemail response, no assistant to pencil you into an overbooked schedule. We serve an on-time God who is not afraid to show up in person at the exact time and location of your crisis.

Matthew 18:18–20 says, "Assuredly, I say to you, whatever you bind on earth will be bound in heaven, and whatever you loose on earth will be loosed in heaven. Again I say to you that if two of you agree on earth concerning anything that they ask, it will be done for them by My Father in heaven. For where two or three are gathered in My name, I am there in the midst of them."

Ladies and gentlemen, this is the greatest instruction manual ever presented, with possibly the easiest directions to follow. God gives us the power to bind Satan and any principalities of darkness that are threatening our life. All we have to do is find a friend and stand in agreement, asking for a resolution in Jesus's name. This request is much more powerful than any game show that allows you to phone a friend. The person on the other end of this call *can* actually move heaven and earth. When you tell Satan to back off in Jesus's name, he has no choice but to do so. You have released the power of God over your life to protect and direct you (or those you love).

How do we pray and ask God to intervene in our lives? The Bible says not to use vain repetition as the Pharisees did. Why does it say this? Because the Pharisees would gather in public places so that everyone could listen to them praying and marvel at how religious they were. The focus was on the man, not the Creator. Anything that takes the focus off of God is not of God. He will not honor you for putting yourself above Him. He created *you* to honor *Him*, not the other way around.

When I was diagnosed with cancer, I asked for healing only once. I was very specific about what I wanted. I didn't tell God how or when to heal me, but I let Him know that I was definitely, 100 percent in need of supernatural healing in order to survive. After I laid this out very clearly, I began to thank God for the healing that was on the way. That didn't mean I knew where this cancer journey would take me; it just meant that I trusted God to lead me down the path He had designed for me.

GET SPECIFIC

When I pray, I am very specific. This way God knows exactly what I'm expecting (not that He doesn't already know my need, but He knows that I'm turning the need over to Him) and I know exactly when God has answered my prayer. If I specifically ask for a thick, black coat with silver buttons down the front to keep me warm in the winter, and my next-door neighbor comes to my house and says she is cleaning out her closet and thought I might like to have her new one she never wore last season...I know this is God working through my neighbor.

When I am specific with my request, there is no doubt that God intervened when my answer shows up wearing a giant red bow. It wasn't my neighbor's blind idea but a prayer that set a series of blessings into motion—blessings for myself and for my neighbor.

Allow me to share a personal example on being specific. When my youngest daughter, Kassidee, was beginning second grade, I was having difficulty teaching her to be responsible for her belongings: backpack, homework, school sweater, glasses, tennis shoes... It wasn't a lot to ask of an eight-year-old, and certainly not an outlandish request. Kassi needed to know she was old enough to corral a few of her own personal items instead of relying on me to constantly keep track.

Her teacher, Mrs. Humbert, is a wonderful woman with the patience of a saint. I explained that I was trying to instill more responsibility in my child, who on any given day would leave her head on the school bus if it wasn't attached to her neck. After many failed attempts on my part, Mrs. Humbert finally asked if I would allow her to hold Kassi in from recess for a few minutes to write lines. I would have asked Kassi to rewrite the Preamble AND the Constitution if it would help; I was just that tired of keeping track of her stuff.

That afternoon Mrs. Humbert asked Kassidee to remain at her desk for a few minutes at the beginning of recess and write lines while the other children filed out of the room and headed straight for the playground. Completely unfazed (and probably a little baffled at the assignment, as this was the first time she was asked to write lines), Kassi was given these instructions. "Write down, 'I will be more responsible.' Write lines and fill up the page."

At the top of Kassi's page she wrote, "I will be more responsible." The rest of the page was filled with tiny lines that looked like identical tic marks: | | | | | | | | | | | | | | | | .

Be specific.

THANK GOD LIKE YOU MEAN IT

The story of the ten lepers in Luke 17:11–19 captures one of the main staples in an effective prayer life—being sure to give God thanks for what He has done. Many of us are guilty of crying out to God when we have a problem, letting Him fix it, then going on our merry way. Things start going well, and we forget to give thanks.

The ten lepers found Jesus and asked Him to have mercy on them. They were living in physical agony and desperately needed His healing touch. Jesus's response is so remarkable because He did absolutely nothing. He didn't lay one finger on them. He didn't pray for them. He didn't have a healing service right there in the middle of the street. He simply told them to go see the priest. That was what you did in Jesus's time when you were healed of a disease, to confirm the healing.

They did as Jesus asked, and because of their obedience they were healed. All ten were healed without so much as a wink from Jesus, and only *one* came back to thank Him. One lone leper (say that fast ten times) returned, fell on his face, and glorified Jesus for healing his body.

Jesus said, "Your faith has made you well." And because this leper worshipped the Lord and followed the instructions Jesus gave him, blessings followed him for the rest of his life. Scripture records that through this great act of obedience he gained supernatural blessings in this life and the life to come.

It almost makes you wish you could do one of those TV specials on the others: "Where are they now?" to follow up with them in their latter days.

Saying thank you to someone is never wasted effort. These are two of the most powerful words in our vocabulary, always appreciated by the recipient. Praising God is one of the commands mentioned consistently throughout the Bible. If we want to see the power of the Master activated in our lives to move those seemingly impossible problems out of our way, we must remember to praise God like there is no tomorrow. The Bible says that God inhabits the praises of His people. David talks about praising Him in song and dance. But the bottom line is, whatever *your* preferred style, stop thinking about yourself for a few seconds and praise the Lord. This invites the Holy Spirit to invade your space and lift you to a place of serenity and worship.

PRAYERS OF BLESSING

One prayer that I love is often used as a blessing at the end of many church services.

Now may the Lord bless you and keep you. May the Lord make His face shine upon you and be gracious unto you. May the Lord lift up His countenance unto you and grant you peace.

Many times clergymen tag on their own specialized endings to tailor-make a blessing for their particular audience. Having heard this preamble to the blessing for most of my life, I wanted to discover its origin. Surely there was a deeper meaning to this prayer. I contacted my dear friend, Jonathan, whom I originally met many moons ago when we were just children ourselves. Now we have children of our own and don't get to talk as often as I would like, but he has always been a wonderful friend.

So I e-mailed Jonathan and asked if he could explain to me the Jewish meaning of the phrase "May God's face shine upon you." Because, of course, any time you want to know the real meaning behind something in the Bible, you find a good Jewish friend to iron it out for you.

"May God's face shine upon you" is a blessing that is repeated not only at Shabbat every Saturday by the parents over the children but also during the morning services held each weekday at the temple. At the temple it is given by the *kohein* (or priest, who is covered by a tallit, which we discussed earlier in the book), spoken in a hushed whisper in an elaborate ritual called *duchaning*. It is a very powerful blessing!

This blessing is said at bar/bat mitzvahs and weddings (or other formal family celebrations) and is a trifold blessing that originated with the high priest in Israel. In Hebrew the blessing actually reads, "May G-d's light shine upon you."

How does God's light shine upon you? God's light shines upon you so that (1) you have enough wealth to be secure in your finances, (2) you are spiritually enlightened, and (3) you are spiritually blessed.

So, my prayer of blessing for you is this:

As you continue life's journey, may God's light shine upon you in good times and bad. May you remember the God who keeps Israel neither slumbers nor sleeps (Ps. 121:4). May God grant you greater strength when your path is crooked (Isa. 45:2). May you always know the peace that surpasses understanding (Phil. 4:7) during the dark storms of night. When your circumstances are the bleakest and you are at your weakest, may Jehovah God grant you unmerited mercy and grace as you learn to trust in the One whom even the winds and the waves obey. May He comfort you when you are alone and guide you when you are at a fork in life's road. May your children be blessed, and may we never forget that the glory is His alone.

Heavenly Father,

Thank You for hearing our prayers. Thank You for giving us the Lord's Prayer and teaching us how to pray in Your Word. May we learn how to honor You with our words and deeds and how to listen to Your answers ... without editing them. You have promised to meet all of our needs according to Your riches in glory. We are truly a needy people who completely rely on You for our very breath. We thank You for the amazing luxury of going straight to the throne room of God with our requests, no middle man required. We ask that You forgive our sins and hear us when we come before You. May Your light shine so brightly in our lives that all those around us see an example of Your love shining through us.

In Jesus's name, amen.

Epilogue

WITH GOD ALL THINGS ARE POSSIBLE

Jesus looked at them and said, "With
man this is impossible, but not with God;
all things are possible with God."
—MARK 10:27, NIV

YOU HAVE HEARD about the various celebrations surrounding my five-year cancer-free checkup and the many prayers I prayed leading up to my healing. You have read snippets of my cancer journey. Now follow me through that special landmark weekend where God whispered in my ear, "*I have been right beside you all along.*"

I was driving in my car from San Antonio to Houston, holding in my hands the thick packet of information MD Anderson had sent for my five-year checkup. This was a collective list of appointments/tests I would attend to celebrate reaching the pinnacle of my treatment to date—being cancer free for five years. The five-year mark is like the Holy Grail for cancer patients, better than winning any lottery. The feeling of total elation just doesn't get any better than this.

I could hardly wait to see those three letters on my chart—NED (no evidence of disease).

As I quickly leafed through pages of medical instruction discussing the tests, times, and dates of my appointments and various bits of paperwork that need to be updated, my brain kicked into rapid-fire memory mode:

> One day I'm like every other busy mother of two young girls, whose biggest concerns are caring for her children and paying bills on time. I'm shuffling through paperwork on my desk and trying to remember online passwords to access information vital to my work week. I'm driving to gymnastics, the vet's office, the pediatrician's office, and stopping by Target to do some grocery shopping. Time to tackle the mountain of laundry. Ah, the glamour!
>
> Then I walk into my own doctor's office with bronchitis and find out just a few short weeks later that I have cancer. This bit of information was shared with me over the phone while driving down the highway. "You have leiomyosarcoma. I have never seen this in my practice before, so you need to contact a specialist right away."
>
> Total shock and disbelief. Life as I know it is over. I am surrounded by uncertainty and grace at the very same time. As I walk into Target this time, a complete stranger approaches me to deliver a message—everything is going to be just fine.
>
> I drive to my first appointment at MD Anderson, the cancer mecca in Houston, Texas, that rates number one for sarcoma treatment in the world. I am blessed to get in so quickly and to find a world-class cancer center so close to home. At the same time I am crushed by the weight of my emotions

and a seemingly endless list of unanswered questions that continually wrap around my brain and split into a thousand different chaotic directions.

Where does my life go from here? Is my life over before it has even really begun? I cannot concentrate past this moment. One day at a time. One hour at a time. Holding my breath.

The news of my cancer begins to leak out, and the grapevine kicks into overdrive. People start calling and e-mailing, asking if I'm going to live or die. There is an undeniable elephant in every room that I enter, something so blatantly obvious it cannot be avoided. There is no escaping this cancer demon; it seeps into every conversation. I am surrounded by pity on every side, hating that complete strangers have totally given up on me.

After one week of testing every cell in my body, my team of doctors at MD Anderson begins to map out a treatment program for me. What if the treatment doesn't work? What will happen to my kids? I try to keep my head above the raging waterline of questions that wants to drown me in the unknown.

I am not afraid of what will happen to me but so concerned with the future of my two girls. I don't look or feel sick. How could this be happening when I look the same as I did yesterday?

My dad announces to our church family that I am fighting cancer and asks them to pray for me. The rumor mill comes to a halt as the prayer request is forwarded around the world. Focusing on the negative possibilities is not an option. I am more than a conqueror!

I move to Houston in order to receive radiation treatments for five incredibly long weeks that seem to last a lifetime. Time stands still, as if I'm traveling at lightning speed and yet not moving at all. I am surrounded by people who are literally dying before my very eyes. I wonder if those who don't return to finish their treatments have gone on to a better place, or if they are simply too sick to come back for more of the same.

Six weeks of rest and then back to MD Anderson for an 11.5-hour surgery. My right leg is reconstructed and any remaining cancer cells are cut out as three teams of doctors remove everything down to the bone. Two days later I finally hear the words that we have all been waiting months to hear, "You are cancer free."

My dad announces in church that the surgery was a complete success, thanking everyone for their prayers. I can still see the radiant smile on his face as he tells me about the announcement, the look of seeing God's grace walk into your life when you absolutely cannot live without it. "There was thunderous applause when I told them [the church audience]." I can see my friends and family members as they find out and start sharing the news of God's unbelievable mercy.

Since hearing the words "cancer free," I have been on my knees, thanking God for every great day, every miserable day, and every crazy day in between. Every day that I am given is a gift I share with my beautiful girls, a gift I will never again take for granted.

I was still daydreaming in my car, driving miles that sped silently by under my tires as I marked the distance from San Antonio to Houston for what seemed like the one-millionth time. The sights and signs on the sides of the road were like old friends welcoming me back. It was as if they knew this was my victory lap. I made it!

Who wants to be counted among the statistics? I do! STATISTICS in my mind stands for:

S—Still
T—Through
A—Amazing
T—Turmoil
I
S—Stand
T—To
I—Inherit
C—Christ's
S—Salvation

Hallelujah!

Isaiah 53:5 says, "But He was wounded for our transgressions, He was bruised for our iniquities: the chastisement for our peace was upon Him; and by His stripes we are healed."

My sins, my sickness, my disease, every bad thing within and around me was conquered the moment Christ took my place on Calvary's cross. I was redeemed and washed whiter than snow. My cancer was defeated before the first cell even started growing. This is what the five-year mark represented for me, salvation from death and disease. I was given a second chance at life because someone else willingly gave up their own.

God had saved me in my greatest hour of need (Jer. 33:3). I couldn't even begin to wrap my brain around the amazing miracles God had brought me through in five short years. At one point I was so sick that I couldn't drive my children anywhere. But on this day we were driving hundreds of miles together to celebrate one of life's sweetest victories.

The best part of this road trip was that my girls remained completely oblivious to this grand cause for celebration. Every trip to them is like a mini-vacation. Because I did not spend time focusing on the toll cancer can take, my children did not know how miraculous my recovery really was.

Cancer is a family disease. It is something that one physical body harbors but consumes everybody that is a part of your family. If a member of your family has cancer, everyone bears the burden. It's like a ticking bomb waiting to explode.

Watching the pain on faces around me was one of the most difficult parts of being a cancer patient. There were no words to make it better, no smile to wash it all away. There were only medical hoops to jump through and prayers to send up asking God to make a way through a very dark valley. This is why I was so elated that my children were too young to carry this burden with me. To them I was just mom. I wasn't sick. I just had a broken leg. I did not have to watch the agony etch itself into their tiny faces. And that was a monumental blessing all its own.

When you look for the smallest blessing, you will not be distracted by even the biggest demon.

I continued driving along, lost in thought. I was overwhelmed by God's continuous faithfulness throughout my life and in the lives of my family members.

My oldest daughter, Mckenzie, was in the passenger seat right next to me, flipping through the pages of a magazine as if she didn't have a care in the world. Ironically I was doing the same thing when I was on my way to MD Anderson for the first time. It seemed like just yesterday and like a distant lifetime ago. Where had the time gone? Kassidee, my youngest daughter, was in the backseat half asleep, wrapped in her soft, pink blanket that had been attached to her since birth. She was wrapped in a cocoon of innocent bliss.

As I watched the mile markers fly by from San Antonio to Houston, I was reminded of the countless times I had traveled this road in my lifetime. As a child I came for the blazing hot Texas summers to visit my grandparents. (This is my grandmother who is mentioned in an early chapter as having conquered her own cancer.)

As an adult, I have burned up this same stretch of highway on my way back and forth from my house to MD Anderson. Some years I visited four times, others eight. This landmark appointment would mean I could change my appointment status to "annual." They would only have the luxury of seeing me once a year. I could already see the heavens parting and hear the angels singing. I expected nothing less than perfect results. The promise of healing that God had given me five years ago was coming full circle.

As the girls and I pulled into the hotel parking lot, I could feel peace drenching us with the comfort of a rain cloud in the middle of a drought. When God gives you a promise, it is the ultimate booster shot. There is no higher form of self-confidence than God delivering a personalized message that will lift you to a place of praise and clarity. No one can steal that moment. No disease can tarnish it.

It was June, and one of the hottest summers on record. If

you have ever experienced the summer heat in Texas where humidity hits you in the face like a wave at the beach before dripping down your back, you know that it's a God thing to feel peace as you are schlepping your luggage through an outdoor parking lot with two kids in tow after listening to an hour of "Are we there yet?" I was totally psyched! Every step was taking me closer to my goal of perfect test results, a testimony of God's exceptional handiwork.

Once encased within the ice-cold confines of our hotel room, the night passed quickly as we ordered dinner and the girls unpacked their Barbies. As I looked around the room I couldn't help but think, "We've come a long way, baby!" Just five years ago my cancer journey was bursting at the seams with uncertainty. No one could tell me where this unexpected road would take me, or if my story was coming to an abrupt and unexpected end. All I had in my arsenal was the promise of healing God had given me and prayer warriors constantly lifting me up. This was more than enough, as little is much when God is in it.

The Bible says that if we have faith the size of a mustard seed, God will move the mountains that stand in our way (Matt. 17:20).

I started saying out loud, "Thank You, God! Thank You for healing me. Thank You for loving me. Thank You for Your mercy. Thank You for Your kindness. Thank You for Your promises that never fail. Thank You for healing me. Thank You for sending Your Son to die for me. Thank You for healthy babies. Thank You!" I continued thanking Him for everything that popped into my mind. And I thanked Him out loud so that I could let my children know how very blessed we are (Prov. 22:6). God's abundance is never some-thing to be taken lightly.

Psalm 136:1 says, "Oh, give thanks to the LORD, for He is good! For His mercy endures forever." Verses 2 and 3 say the same thing. The idea is . . . to give thanks.

After I explained to the girls why we need to be thankful for the blessings in our lives, we laid our clothes out and I gave last-minute instructions for the following day. My oldest daughter would love for each day to begin with a printed card of times and activities because she relishes structure. My youngest daughter couldn't care less. Either way, I wanted them to know what to expect when they woke up.

Tucking them in to the overstuffed hotel bed next to mine, it took awhile for me to nod off. I love to sink into the soft confines of luxurious hotel sheets, but I simply could not stop thanking God for His mercy, for His love, and for sending His Son to die for me. Had God not spared my life, I simply would not be relaxing in a warm, comfy bed watching my daughters drift off into peaceful slumber, I would be in a cemetery somewhere pushing up daisies.

The sheer excitement of how much God had done in my life kept me awake for most of the night. Just five years ago the thought of being in this amazing place of total healing was a dream. Today my dream was coming true.

Of course, before I knew it the phone was jangling with the automated and oh-so-personal wake-up call. We were off. Our backpacks loaded with snacks and games, we were ready to face the long day ahead of us. As we walked in the front door and I checked the girls in at the MD Anderson information desk, we headed to the first testing area.

Having navigated this complex system of winding hallways for several years, I knew exactly where to go. The walkways were no longer intimidating. At this point I could have given guided tours.

After my first round of tests I was running short on time before my next set began, so I was somewhat distracted as I tried to make up my time by walking quickly to the next waiting room. I felt badly that I didn't even notice the lady walking right up behind me as I was setting a pace that almost set the carpet on fire. I was just in the zone, ready to take my tests and hear spectacular results.

"You're Pastor Hagee's daughter, aren't you? I saw you share your story on TV." I had to laugh because I'm sure I looked like a hot mess, wearing scrubs with medical tape strapped up and down my arms to cover the needle marks. I was surprised she even recognized me at all. With any luck I appeared slightly more glamorous in real life than I did at this particular moment in time.

I looked up and gave her a genuine smile, knowing that if she was at MD Anderson, she was either battling cancer herself or sitting with a loved one facing the fight of their life. I quickly noticed she was wearing street clothes and had no medical bracelets or insignia. Before the words came out of her mouth, I knew she was here with a friend or family member. I could see the familiar pain in her eyes that comes with holding on to a hardship that you can do nothing to control or contain.

"I'm here with my husband, who has prostate cancer." I felt the familiar sting of painful words shared by someone facing this impossible disease. I looked into her eyes and listened to her story. As much as I hate running late, my appointment would have to wait. "I watch your dad on TV and heard your testimony of how God healed you. Please pray for my husband."

I was absolutely honored to do so, and I assured her that God is not a respecter of persons (Acts 10:34). What He had done for me, He could certainly do for her husband. I hated that I didn't have more time to spend with her, but she found me on Facebook and updated me on her husband's status later in the week. I have no doubt that God will give them their own victory.

The rest of the day flew by in a flurry of tests, shuttle rides, and the usual amount of hospital paperwork. Before I knew it, I was sitting in my oncologist's office waiting to hear the test results. Years of testing and surgeries boiled down to this one shining moment. Bring it on, baby! I was ready!

MD Anderson has the very latest in medical technology. When you take a test there, the results can be read the same day, usually within the hour. The entire hospital is on the same computer system, so the tech uploads the X-ray, film, or test results, which are then verified by a second set of doctors or radiologists. The oncologist is then ready to relay the results to the patient, literally within minutes of their being uploaded onto the hospital's computer system. I love ridiculously fast technology!

As I sat in the lobby, waiting for my final appointment of the day, I was hardly able to contain my excitement. I felt like pulling a Tom Cruise and jumping up and down on the couch. I felt like clapping my hands and screaming for joy! I was ecstatic to be in this cancer center, celebrating a day of complete victory!

The nurse checked my weight for the fourth time that day, and I was starting to grow a little weary with having my blood pressure checked, but nothing could steal this moment from me. Of course my blood pressure was up! I was excited. I needed a cheeseburger and was tired of needles. I just wanted to get my results and return to the hotel for a celebratory dinner.

Could we please get on with this?

Finally tucked away in an exam room, I waited (not so patiently) as the first doctor came in. Since MD Anderson is part of the University of Texas system and a teaching hospital, it is almost guaranteed that your doctor or nurse will be shadowed by more than one student who is studying to become some type of cancer doctor, nurse, or technician. You answer the same questions over and over and over again.

The first doctor in today's lineup came in and asked me, in a painfully professional voice, how I had been feeling and if I had been experiencing any problems. I immediately knew that he was a student because he was very serious and furiously writing notes on his pad as if his very life depended upon my answers to his rote questions that he had probably already asked fifty times that day. After he was satisfied, he excused himself with a quick, "Dr. Moon will be in to see you shortly."

"Shortly," in a hospital, is a relative term. I grabbed my phone and started responding to e-mails when the door swung open and in walked Dr. Moon, my lead oncologist. This was the man who was going to announce my flawless test results. Had they rolled out a red carpet for his entrance and started sounding a celebratory trumpet, it would not have been out of line. This was a red letter day.

Towering over me, Dr. Moon leaned down to shake my hand and tell me that he didn't see anything to be concerned about on my tests (translation, "no cancer was found in your body"). And just like that, it was finished. The battle was over.

"When's the party?" I could hear Dr. Moon asking me questions about how I was going to celebrate. He was fighting for space in my head that was screaming THANK YOU to God for healing me, to those who prayed for me, to my family who stood by me, to my husband who had to take on extra tasks when I was unable to lend a hand, and to my girls who continue to put a smile on my face every day. I was singing a hundred songs at the same time, but the one that took me by surprise was the one I heard as I entered the cab on my way back to the hotel.

Clinging tightly to the good news I had just received for the precious gift that it is, the girls and I head out the front door of the hospital and waited for our turn at the cab station. I could hardly keep from shouting! I wanted everyone to know the great things God had done for me.

Finally it was our turn, and I opened the cab door, ready for the short ride to the hotel. I was floating on a cloud, not really paying attention to what was going on around me as I feverishly texted the good news to my friends and relatives. I could not type the words fast enough.

Then it smacked me in the face. The song the Jamaican cab driver was blasting in his cab was "It Is Well With My Soul." This wasn't background music. The volume was set so high that I almost had to yell the directions to my hotel over the island beat. I had never heard this rendition of the song, but I was completely moved by the enormity of the message.

On the five-minute drive to the hotel the cab driver told me the story of Horatio Spafford and his hymn that has touched countless lives. I let him tell me the story, even though I know it by heart and could fill in details he had omitted. I was lost in the fact that God would take one more opportunity to remind me (on my way out of the hospital, in a not-so-random cab) that everything was going to be just fine. I could almost hear God whispering, "I told you so."

It was—and is—indeed, well with my soul.

You may be facing an impossible situation of your own. But I want you to know today that no matter what people say to you, focus on God and the promises in His Word. Get in a quiet place, worship, open your Bible, and listen for His voice. What men say cannot limit what God can do. He is your healer. He is your provider. He is your way maker. He is faithful and will not let you down. An impossible situation is the perfect environment for God to supernaturally intervene. Don't be ruled by doubt or fear. Have faith in God. He will master the impossible in your life.

Appendix

SCRIPTURES TO HELP YOU
MASTER THE IMPOSSIBLE

SOMETIMES LIFE SENDS us through scenarios that sear us to the very bone. Every fiber of our being is affected, and we are left reeling from circumstances beyond our control. The good news is that God is still large and in charge. He can heal broken hearts, broken homes, financial disasters, and everything in between. Pulling us from the depths of our very worst, unspeakable tragedy is just the beginning of the many miracles He can perform for us today!

If you are looking to make a remarkable difference in your life, saturate your day with Scripture. Find those verses that speak to your situation specifically, and post them throughout your home. Speak them out loud. The spoken Word is a very powerful tool that will give you unlimited potential through Jesus Christ. You will find no greater source of knowledge to help you through your personal tragedy, no quicker way to become triumphant than to use Scripture as your first line of defense.

Here are just a few verses to get you started, and as you find some of your own, feel free to add them or highlight them in your Bible. With these power tools you can begin to construct your own road map for tackling the over-whelming obstacles currently standing in your way. God bless you on your way to total victory!

Old Testament

Exodus

The LORD will fight for you, and you shall hold your peace.

—Exodus 14:14

If you diligently heed the voice of the LORD your God and do what is right in His sight, give ear to His commandments and keep all His statutes, I will put none of the diseases on you which I have brought on the Egyptians. For I am the LORD who heals you.

—Exodus 15:26

Deuteronomy

So it shall be, when the LORD your God brings you into the land of which He swore to your fathers, to Abraham, Isaac, and Jacob, to give you large and beautiful cities which you did not build, houses full of all good things, which you did not fill, hewn-out wells which you did not dig, vineyards and olive trees which you did not plant—when you have eaten and are full—then beware, lest you forget the LORD who brought you out of the land of Egypt, from the house of bondage.

—Deuteronomy 6:10–12

I call heaven and earth as witnesses today against you, that I have set before you life and death, blessing and cursing; therefore choose life, that both you and your descendants may live; that you may love the LORD your God, that you may obey His voice, and that you may cling to Him, for He is your life and the length of your days.

—DEUTERONOMY 30:19

1 Samuel

Then David said to the Philistine, "You come to me with a sword, with a spear, and with a javelin. But I come to you in the name of the LORD of hosts, the God of the armies of Israel, whom you have defied.... The battle is the LORD's."

—1 SAMUEL 17:45, 47

2 Samuel

The LORD is my rock and my fortress and my
    deliverer;
The God of my strength, in whom I will trust;
My shield and the horn of my salvation,
My stronghold and my refuge;
My Savior, You save me from violence.
I will call upon the LORD, who is worthy to be
    praised;
So shall I be saved from my enemies.

—2 SAMUEL 22:2–4

1 Chronicles

Oh, give thanks to the LORD, for He is good!
For His mercy endures forever.

—1 CHRONICLES 16:34

> Yours, O LORD, is the greatness,
> The power and the glory,
> The victory and the majesty;
> For all that is in heaven and in earth is Yours;
> Yours is the kingdom, O LORD,
> And You are exalted as head over all.
>
> —1 CHRONICLES 29:11

2 Chronicles

> If My people who are called by My name will humble themselves, and pray and seek My face, and turn from their wicked ways, then I will hear from heaven, and will forgive their sin and heal their land.
>
> —2 CHRONICLES 7:14

Job

> You have granted me life and favor,
> And Your care has preserved my spirit.
>
> —JOB 10:12

Psalms

> LORD, how they have increased who trouble me!
> Many are those who rise up against me.
> Many are they who say of me,
> "There is no help for him in God."
> But You, O LORD, are a shield for me,
> My glory and the One who lifts up my head.
>
> —PSALM 3:1–3

> Therefore my heart is glad, and my glory rejoices;
> My flesh also will rest in hope....

You will show me the path of life;
In your presence is fullness of joy;
At your right hand are pleasures forevermore.
—PSALM 16:9, 11

Yea, though I walk through the valley of the
    shadow of death,
I will fear no evil;
For You *are* with me;
Your rod and Your staff, they comfort me.
—PSALM 23:4

Hear the voice of my supplications
When I cry to You,
When I lift up my hands toward Your holy
    sanctuary.
—PSALM 28:2

I will extol You, O LORD, for You have lifted me
    up,
And have not let my foes rejoice over me.
O LORD my God, I cried out to You,
And You healed me....
For His anger is but for a moment,
His favor is for life;
Weeping may endure for a night,
But joy comes in the morning.
—PSALM 30:1–2, 5

I will bless the LORD at all times;
His praise *shall* continually *be* in my mouth.
—PSALM 34:1

The steps of a good man are ordered by the LORD,
And He delights in his way.
Though he fall, he shall not be utterly cast down;
For the Lord upholds him with His hand.
I have been young, and now am old;
Yet I have not seen the righteous forsaken,
Nor his descendants begging bread.
He is ever merciful, and lends;
And his descendants are blessed.
Depart from evil, and do good;
And dwell forevermore.
For the LORD loves justice,
And does not forsake His saints;
They are preserved forever,
But the descendants of the wicked shall be cut off.
The righteous shall inherit the land,
And dwell in it forever.

—PSALM 37:23–29

And now, Lord, what do I wait for?
My hope is in you.
Deliver me from all my transgressions;
Do not make me the reproach of the foolish.

—PSALM 39:7–8

I waited patiently for the Lord;
And He inclined to me,
And heard my cry.
He also brought me up out of a horrible pit,
Out of the miry clay,
And set my feet upon a rock,
And established my steps.
He has put a new song in my mouth—
Praise to our God;

Many will see it and fear,
And will trust in the LORD.

—PSALM 40:1–3

Why are you cast down, O my soul?
And why are you disquieted within me?
Hope in God;
For I shall yet praise Him,
The help of my countenance and my God.

—PSALM 42:11

Be still, and know that I am God;
I will be exalted among the nations,
I will be exalted in the earth!
The LORD of hosts is with us;
The God of Jacob is our refuge.

—PSALM 46:10–11

Oh, clap your hands, all you peoples!
Shout to God with the voice of triumph!

—PSALM 47:1

Call upon Me in the day of trouble;
I will deliver you, and you shall glorify Me.

—PSALM 50:15

Create in me a clean heart, O God,
And renew a steadfast spirit within me.
Do not cast me away from Your presence,
And do not take Your Holy Spirit from me.
Restore to me the joy of Your salvation,
And uphold me by Your generous Spirit.

—PSALM 51:10–12

Cast your burden on the LORD,
And He shall sustain you;
He shall never permit the righteous to be moved.
—PSALM 55:22

Whenever I am afraid,
I will trust in You.
—PSALM 56:3

He shall send from heaven and save me;
He reproaches the one who would swallow me up.
God shall send forth His mercy and His truth.
—PSALM 57:3

For Your mercy reaches unto the heavens,
And Your truth unto the clouds.
Be exalted, O God, above the heavens;
Let Your glory be above all the earth.
—PSALM 57:10–11

My soul, wait silently for God alone,
For my expectation is from Him.
He only is my rock and my salvation;
He is my defense;
I shall not be moved.
In God is my salvation and my glory;
The rock of my strength,
And my refuge, is in God.
Trust in Him at all times, you people;
Pour out your heart before Him;
God is a refuge for us.
—PSALM 62:5–8

Because Your lovingkindness is better than life,
My lips shall praise You.
Thus I will bless You while I live;
I will lift up my hands in Your name.
My soul shall be satisfied as with marrow and
    fatness,
And my mouth shall praise You with joyful lips.
—Psalm 63:3–5

Oh, bless our God, you peoples! And make the
    voice of His praise to be heard,
Who keeps our soul among the living,
And does not allow our feet to be moved.
For You, O God, have tested us;
You have refined us as silver is refined.
You brought us into the net;
You laid affliction on our backs.
You have caused men to ride over our heads;
We went through fire and through water;
But you brought us out to rich fulfillment.
—Psalm 66:8–12

Deliver me, O my God, out of the hand of the
    wicked,
Out of the hand of the unrighteous and cruel man.
For You are my hope, O Lord God;
You are my trust from my youth.
—Psalm 71:4–5

Bless the Lord, O my soul;
And all that is within me, bless His holy name!
Bless the Lord, O my soul,
And forget not all His benefits:
Who forgives all your iniquities,

Who heals all your diseases,
Who redeems your life from destruction,
Who crowns you with lovingkindness and tender
    mercies,
Who satisfies your mouth with good things,
So that your youth is renewed like the eagle's.
       —PSALM 103:1–5

Let the redeemed of the LORD say so,
Whom He has redeemed from the hand of the
    enemy . . .
       —PSALM 107:2

The fear of the LORD is the beginning of wisdom;
A good understanding have all those who do His
    commandments.
His praise endures forever.
       —PSALM 111:10

Oh, give thanks to the LORD, for He is good!
For His mercy endures forever.
       —PSALM 118:1

I shall not die, but live,
And declare the works of the LORD.
The LORD has chastened me severely,
But He has not given me over to death.
       —PSALM 118:17–18

This is the day the LORD has made;
We will rejoice and be glad in it.
       —PSALM 118:24

Your word is a lamp to my feet
And a light to my path.

—PSALM 119:105

I rise before the dawning of the morning,
And cry for help;
I hope in Your word.

—PSALM 119:147

Consider my affliction and deliver me,
For I do not forget Your law.

—PSALM 119:153

Those who trust in the LORD
Are like Mount Zion,
Which cannot be moved, but abides forever.
As the mountains surround Jerusalem,
So the LORD surrounds His people
From this time forth and forever.

—PSALM 125:1–2

Out of the depths I have cried to You, O LORD;
Lord, hear my voice!
Let Your ears be attentive
To the voice of my supplications.
If You, LORD, should mark iniquities,
O Lord, who could stand?
But there is forgiveness with You,
That You may be feared.
I wait for the LORD, my soul waits,
And in His word I do hope.

—PSALM 130:1–5

Oh, give thanks to the LORD, for He is good!
For His mercy endures forever.

—PSALM 136:1

The LORD will perfect that which concerns me;
Your mercy, O LORD, endures forever;
Do not forsake the works of Your hands.

—PSALM 138:8

Where can I go from Your Spirit?
Or where can I flee from Your presence?
If I ascend into heaven, You are there;
If I make my bed in hell, behold, You are there.
If I take the wings of the morning,
And dwell in the uttermost parts of the sea,
Even there Your hand shall lead me,
And Your right hand shall hold me.

—PSALM 139:7–10

I also recommend that you read Psalms 27, 61, 91, 100, and 121 in their entirety.

Proverbs

A good man obtains favor from the LORD,
But a man of wicked intentions he will condemn.

—PROVERBS 12:2

Anxiety in the heart of man causes depression,
But a good word makes it glad.
The righteous should choose his friends carefully,
For the way of the wicked leads them astray.

—PROVERBS 12:25–26

Train up a child in the way he should go,
And when he is old he will not depart from it.

—PROVERBS 22:6

Ecclesiastes

I know that whatever God does,
It shall be forever.
Nothing can be added to it,
And nothing taken from it.

—ECCLESIASTES 3:14

The words of a wise man's mouth are gracious,
But the lips of a fool shall swallow him up.

—ECCLESIASTES 10:12

Isaiah

You will keep him in perfect peace,
Whose mind is stayed on You,
Because he trusts in You.

—ISAIAH 26:3

I will give you the treasures of darkness
And hidden riches of secret places,
That you may know that I, the LORD,
Who call you by your name,
Am the God of Israel.

—ISAIAH 45:3

But He was wounded for our transgressions,
He was bruised for our iniquities;
The chastisement for our peace was upon Him,
And by His stripes we are healed.

—ISAIAH 53:5

"No weapon formed against you shall prosper,
And every tongue which rises against you in
judgment
You shall condemn.
This is the heritage of the servants of the LORD,
And their righteousness is from Me,"
Says the LORD.

—ISAIAH 54:17

"For My thoughts are not your thoughts,
Nor are your ways My ways," says the LORD.
"For as the heavens are higher than the earth,
So are My ways higher than your ways,
And my thoughts than your thoughts.
For as the rain comes down, and the snow from
heaven,
And do not return there,
But water the earth,
And make it bring forth and bud,
That it may give seed to the sower
And bread to the eater,
So shall My word be that goes forth from My
mouth;
It shall not return to Me void,
But it shall accomplish what I please,
And it shall prosper in the thing for which I sent
it."

—ISAIAH 55:8–11

Jeremiah

Before I formed you in the womb I knew you;
Before you were born I sanctified you.

—JEREMIAH 1:5

Blessed is the man who trusts in the LORD,
And whose hope is in the LORD.
For he shall be like a tree planted by the waters,
Which spreads out its roots by the river,
And will not fear when heat comes;
But its leaf will be green,
And will not be anxious in the year of drought,
Nor will cease from yielding fruit.

—JEREMIAH 17:7

For I know the thoughts that I think toward you, says the LORD, thoughts of peace and not of evil, to give you a future and a hope. Then you will call upon Me and go and pray to Me, and I will listen to you. And you will seek Me and find Me, when you search for Me with all your heart.

—JEREMIAH 29:11–13

Lamentations

Through the LORD's mercies we are not consumed,
Because His compassions fail not.
They are new every morning;
Great is Your faithfulness.
"The LORD is my portion," says my soul,
"Therefore I hope in Him!"
The LORD is good to those who wait for Him,
To the soul who seeks Him.
It is good that one should hope and wait quietly
For the salvation of the LORD.

—LAMENTATIONS 3:22–26

Ezekiel

> I will make them and the places all around My hill
> a blessing; and I will cause showers to come down
> in their season; there shall be showers of blessing.
>
> —EZEKIEL 34:26

Daniel

> Then he said to me, "Do not fear, Daniel, for from
> the first day that you set your heart to understand,
> and to humble yourself before your God, your
> words were heard; and I have come because of your
> words."
>
> —DANIEL 10:12

> Blessed is he who waits...
>
> —DANIEL 12:12

Joel

> So I will restore to you the years that the
>   swarming locust has eaten,
> The crawling locust,
> The consuming locust,
> And the chewing locust,
> My great army which I sent among you.
> You shall eat in plenty and be satisfied,
> And praise the name of the LORD your God,
> Who has dealt wondrously with you;
> And My people shall never be put to shame.
> Then you shall know that I am in the midst of
>   Israel;

I am the LORD your God
And there is no other.
My people shall never be put to shame.

—JOEL 2:25–27

Amos

For thus says the LORD to the house of Israel: "Seek Me and live."

—AMOS 5:4

Micah

Therefore I will look to the LORD;
I will wait for the God of my salvation;
My God will hear me.

—MICAH 7:7

Nahum

The LORD is slow to anger and great in power...

—NAHUM 1:3

Habakkuk

Then the LORD answered me and said: "Write the vision and make it plain on tablets, that he may run who reads it."

—HABAKKUK 2:2

Zechariah

"Not by might nor by power, but by My Spirit,"
Says the LORD of hosts.

—ZECHARIAH 4:6

NEW TESTAMENT

Matthew But seek first the kingdom of God and His righteousness, and all these things shall be added to you. Therefore do not worry about tomorrow, for tomorrow will worry about its own things. Sufficient for the day is its own trouble.

—MATTHEW 6:33–34

If you then, being evil, know how to give good gifts to your children, how much more will your Father who is in heaven give good things to those who ask Him!

—MATTHEW 7:11

And I will give you the keys of the kingdom of heaven, and whatever you bind on earth will be bound in heaven, and whatever you loose on earth will be loosed in heaven.

—MATTHEW 16:19

So Jesus said to them, "...if you have faith as a mustard seed, you will say to this mountain, 'Move from here to there,' and it will move; and nothing will be impossible for you."

—MATTHEW 17:20

For where two or three are gathered together in My name, I am there in the midst of them.

—MATTHEW 18:20

...teaching them to observe all things that I have commanded you; and lo, I am with you always, even to the end of the age.

—Matthew 28:20

Mark

And He said to her, "Daughter, your faith has made you well. Go in peace, and be healed of your affliction."

—Mark 5:34

Luke

Then He called His twelve disciples together and gave them power and authority over all demons, and to cure diseases. He sent them to preach the kingdom of God and to heal the sick.

—Luke 9:1–2

So I say to you, ask, and it will be given to you; seek, and you will find; knock, and it will be opened to you. For everyone who asks receives, and he who seeks finds, and to him who knocks it will be opened. If a son asks for bread from any father among you, will he give him a stone? Or if he asks for a fish, will he give him a serpent instead of a fish? Or if he asks for an egg, will he offer him a scorpion? If you then, being evil, know how to give good gifts to your children, how much more will your heavenly Father give the Holy Spirit to those who ask Him?

—Luke 11:9–13

Do not fear, little flock, for it is your Father's good pleasure to give you the kingdom.

—LUKE 12:32

John

For God so loved the world that He gave His only begotten Son, that whoever believes in Him should not perish but have everlasting life.

—JOHN 3:16

Therefore if the Son makes you free, you shall be free indeed.

—JOHN 8:36

The thief does not come except to steal, and to kill, and to destroy. I have come that they may have life, and that they may have it more abundantly.

—JOHN 10:10

And whatever you ask in My name, that I will do, that the Father may be glorified in the Son.

—JOHN 14:13

Peace I leave with you, My peace I give to you; not as the world gives do I give to you. Let not your heart be troubled, neither let it be afraid.

—JOHN 14:27

Therefore you now have sorrow; but I will see you again and your heart will rejoice, and your joy no one will take from you. And in that day you will ask Me nothing. Most assuredly, I say to you, whatever you ask the Father in My name He will give you. Until now you have asked nothing in My name. Ask, and you will receive, that your joy may be full.

—JOHN 16:22–24

Acts

Then Peter opened his mouth and said: "In truth I perceive that God shows no partiality. But in every nation whoever fears Him and works righteousness is accepted by Him."

—ACTS 10:34–35

Romans

...we also glory in tribulations, knowing that tribulation produces perseverance; and perseverance, character; and character, hope. Now hope does not disappoint, because the love of God has been poured out in our hearts by the Holy Spirit who was given to us.

—ROMANS 5:3–5

Likewise the Spirit also helps in our weaknesses. For we do not know what we should pray for as we ought, but the Spirit Himself makes intercession for us with groanings which cannot be uttered. Now He who searches the hearts knows what the mind of the Spirit is, because He makes intercession for the saints according to the will of God. And we know that all things work together for good to those who love God, to those who are the called according to His purpose.

—ROMANS 8:26–28

What then shall we say to these things? If God is for us, who can be against us?...Yet in all these things we are more than conquerors through Him who loved us.

—Romans 8:31, 37

Let love be without hypocrisy. Abhor what is evil. Cling to what is good. Be kindly affectionate to one another with brotherly love, in honor giving preference to one another; not lagging in diligence, fervent in spirit, serving the Lord; rejoicing in hope, patient in tribulation, continuing steadfastly in prayer; distributing to the needs of the saints, given to hospitality. Bless those who persecute you; bless and do not curse.

—Romans 12:9–14

1 Corinthians

For now we see in a mirror, dimly, but then face to face. Now I know in part, but then I shall know just as I also am known. And now abide faith, hope, love, these three; but the greatest of these is love.

—1 Corinthians 13:12–13

2 Corinthians

We are hard-pressed on every side, yet not crushed; we are perplexed, but not in despair; persecuted, but not forsaken; struck down, but not destroyed...

—2 Corinthians 4:8–9

Therefore we do not lose heart. Even though our outward man is perishing, yet the inward man is being renewed day by day. For our light affliction, which is but for a moment, is working for us in a far more exceeding and eternal weight of glory, while we do not look at the things which are seen, but at the things which are not seen. For the things which are seen are temporary, but the things which are not seen are eternal.

—2 CORINTHIANS 4:16–18

Galatians

And let us not grow weary while doing good, for in due season we shall reap if we do not lose heart. Therefore, as we have opportunity, let us do good to all, especially to those who are of the household of faith.

—GALATIANS 6:9–10

Ephesians

In Him we have redemption through His blood, the forgiveness of sins, according to the riches of His grace.

—EPHESIANS 1:7

For by grace you have been saved through faith, and that not of yourselves; it is the gift of God, not of works, lest anyone should boast. For we are His workmanship, created in Christ Jesus for good works, which God prepared beforehand that we should walk in them.

—EPHESIANS 2:8–10

Therefore I ask that you do not lose heart at my tribulations for you, which is your glory. For this reason I bow my knees to the Father of our Lord

Jesus Christ, from whom the whole family in heaven and earth is named, that He would grant you, according to the riches of His glory, to be strengthened with might through His Spirit in the inner man, that Christ may dwell in your hearts through faith; that you, being rooted and grounded in love, may be able to comprehend with all the saints what is the width and length and depth and height—to know the love of Christ which passes knowledge; that you may be filled with all the fullness of God. Now to Him who is able to do exceedingly abundantly above all that we ask or think, according to the power that works in us, to Him be glory in the church by Christ Jesus to all generations, forever and ever. Amen.

—EPHESIANS 3:13–21

And be kind to one another, tenderhearted, forgiving one another, even as God in Christ forgave you.

—EPHESIANS 4:32

Finally, my brethren, be strong in the Lord and in the power of His might. Put on the whole armor of God, that you may be able to stand against the wiles of the devil. For we do not wrestle against flesh and blood, but against principalities, against powers, against the rulers of the darkness of this age, against spiritual hosts of wickedness in the heavenly places. Therefore take up the whole armor of God, that you may be able to withstand in the evil day, and having done all, to stand.

—EPHESIANS 6:10–13

Philippians

For it is God who works in you both to will and to do for His good pleasure. Do all things without complaining and disputing.

—PHILIPPIANS 2:13–14

I press toward the goal for the prize of the upward call of God in Christ Jesus.

—PHILIPPIANS 3:14

And the peace of God, which surpasses all understanding, will guard your hearts and minds through Christ Jesus.

—PHILIPPIANS 4:7

I can do all things through Christ who strengthens me.

—PHILIPPIANS 4:13

Colossians

You are complete in Him, who is the head of all principality and power.

—COLOSSIANS 2:10

1 Thessalonians

Rejoice always, pray without ceasing, in everything give thanks; for this is the will of God in Christ Jesus for you. Do not quench the Spirit. Do not despise prophecies. Test all things; hold fast what is good. Abstain from every form of evil.

—1 THESSALONIANS 5:16–22

2 Thessalonians

> But the Lord is faithful, who will establish you and guard you from the evil one.
> —2 Thessalonians 3:3

1 Timothy

> But you, O man of God, flee these things and pursue righteousness, godliness, faith, love, patience, gentleness. Fight the good fight of faith, lay hold on eternal life, to which you were also called and have confessed the good confession in the presence of many witnesses.
> —1 Timothy 6:11–12

2 Timothy

> Therefore I remind you to stir up the gift of God which is in you through the laying on of my hands. For God has not given us a spirit of fear, but of power and of love and of a sound mind.
> —2 Timothy 1:6–7

Titus

> For the grace of God that brings salvation has appeared to all men, teaching us that, denying ungodliness and worldly lusts, we should live soberly, righteously, and godly in the present age, looking for the blessed hope and glorious appearing of our great God and Savior Jesus Christ, who gave Himself for us, that He might redeem us from

every lawless deed and purify for Himself His own special people, zealous for good works.

—TITUS 2:11–14

Hebrews

Though He was a Son, yet He learned obedience by the things which He suffered. And having been perfected, He became the author of eternal salvation to all who obey Him.

—HEBREWS 5:8–9

Now faith is the substance of things hoped for, the evidence of things not seen.

—HEBREWS 11:1

Jesus Christ is the same yesterday, today, and forever.

—HEBREWS 13:8

James

But let patience have its perfect work, that you may be perfect and complete, lacking nothing.

—JAMES 1:4

Pray one for another, that you may be healed. The effective, fervent prayer of a righteous man avails much.

—JAMES 5:16

1 Peter

Be sober, be vigilant; because your adversary the devil walks about like a roaring lion, seeking whom he may devour. Resist him, steadfast in the faith, knowing that the same sufferings are experienced by your brotherhood in the world. But may the God of all grace, who called us to His eternal glory by Christ Jesus, after you have suffered a while, perfect, establish, strengthen, and settle you. To Him be the glory and the dominion forever and ever. Amen.

—1 PETER 5:8–11

2 Peter

For we did not follow cunningly devised fables when we made known to you the power and coming of our Lord Jesus Christ, but were eyewitnesses of His majesty. For He received from God the Father honor and glory when such a voice came to Him from the Excellent Glory: "This is My beloved Son, in whom I am well pleased."

—2 PETER 1:16–18

1 John

And this is the promise that He has promised us— eternal life.

—1 JOHN 2:25

By this we know love, because He laid down His life for us. And we also ought to lay down our lives for the brethren. But whoever has this world's goods, and sees his brother in need, and shuts up his heart from him, how does the love of God abide in him? My little children, let us not love in word or in tongue, but in deed and in truth.

—1 JOHN 3:16–18

You are of God, little children, and have overcome them, because He who is in you is greater than he who is in the world.

—1 John 4:4

For whatever is born of God overcomes the world. And this is the victory that has overcome the world—our faith.

—1 John 5:4

2 John

Grace, mercy, and peace will be with you from God the Father and from the Lord Jesus Christ, the Son of the Father, in truth and love.

—2 John 3

3 John

Beloved, I pray that you may prosper in all things and be in health, just as your soul prospers. For I rejoiced greatly when brethren came and testified of the truth that is in you, just as you walk in truth. I have no greater joy than to hear that my children walk in truth.

—3 John 2-4

Jude

To those who are called, sanctified by God the Father, and preserved in Jesus Christ: mercy, peace, and love be multiplied to you.

—Jude 1-2

Revelation

> I am He who lives, and was dead, and behold, I am alive forevermore. Amen. And I have the keys of Hades and Death.
>
> —Revelation 1:18